Good Housekeeping

101 EASY RECIPES
WHEAT-FREE

101 EASY RECIPES
WHEAT-FREE

Lynda Brown

COLLINS & BROWN

First published in United Kingdom in 2006 by
Collins & Brown Limited
151 Freston Road
London W10 6TH

An imprint of Anova Books Company Ltd.

2 3 4 5 6 7 8 9

Project editors: Nicola Hodgson and Carly Madden
Design manager: Gemma Wilson
Production controller: Morna McPherson
Copy editor: Kathy Steer
Nutritional analysis: Jenny McGlyne
Designer: Abby Franklin
Indexer: Michèle Clarke

ISBN 978-1-84340-355-5

A catalogue record for this book is available from the British Library.

Reproduction by Anorax
Printed and bound by Craft Print International Ltd, Singapore

This book can be ordered direct from the publisher.
Contact the marketing department, but try your bookshop first.

www.anovabooks.com

All the ingredients used in this book are readily available. When buying them,
choose local free range or organic when you can. Organic oats, milk carrots,
potatoes and eggs, plus many other staples are available from all supermarkets.
When using zest of oranges or lemons, it's a good idea to also use organic
oranges and lemons. All the recipes in the book are wheat-free; many are also
gluten-free (marked with a green symbol 🌾).

Contents

Foreword

I consider myself lucky – I like all food and it likes me. But we know from your letters, emails and reader queries that there are many of you who can't eat wheat or are cooking for family or friends who have an allergic reaction to food containing wheat. Escalating numbers of people in the UK are finding that they have a wheat intolerance, so I know this book will become a lifeline to many of you. Cutting out all wheat-related products from your diet, doesn't mean you can't still cook delicious and interesting meals. Whether you've just been diagnosed with having an intolerance or have been living with it for a while, this book has everything you need to know. There's a hit list of food you need to avoid and, following it, a list of food that you can eat. Rather than feeling deprived, it's a great chance to discover ingredients you may not have cooked with before. We've gathered together 101 recipes, from energy-boosting breakfasts to quick lunchtime snacks and quick family suppers. There are also some great dinner-party recipes – no one need know it's a wheat-free menu! – and some easy desserts, cakes and biscuits, so you won't feel like you're missing out. Plus all the recipes have been triple tested in the Good Housekeeping kitchens to make sure they work every time. Enjoy!

Emma Marsden
Cookery Editor
Good Houskeeping

Introduction

This book has been written to help the escalating numbers of people who feel they may be intolerant to wheat, for those people who are wheat intolerant or allergic to wheat, and to help everyone who wants to ensure that they enjoy a healthy diet that is easy to prepare and cook. All the recipes in the book are wheat-free and many are also gluten-free (marked with the green symbol 🌾). In addition we have included the nutritional breakdown for every recipe, and ensured that none of the recipes are laden with too many calories.

Many allergy and nutritional specialists believe that a modern diet, with its over-reliance on processed foods, is detrimental to the all round health and vitality that we all seek. There is general consensus too that, though not exclusively so, most food intolerances are primarily a modern disease, a result of the way our diets and the way our food is produced have changed over the last 50 years.

The debate about food intolerances will continue for some time, but there is no doubt that removing the source of a food intolerance or allergy from your diet can change your life. Apart from removing obvious unwanted physical symptoms, energy levels rise, and you can expect to feel brighter, more mentally alert, and more positive in every way. Even if you are not wheat intolerant, adopting a healthy diet and making some simple lifestyle changes can work wonders.

A question often asked is whether wheat-free means low in carbohydrate? The answer is no. Carbohydrates (carbs) are an important energy and mood food, and are an essential part of any healthy eating plan. What is crucial is to eat good carbs, not bad carbs. A normal diet can often contain too much refined wheat (bad carbs) at the expense of complex carbohydrates (good carbs). A wheat-free diet, with its emphasis on complex carbs, redresses this balance, and ensures that your body receives the high-quality carbs it needs. A wheat-free diet is not a faddy diet, or a specific weight-reducing diet. People usually lose weight on a wheat-free diet because their diet becomes better and contains more fresh, filling foods and processed foods and snacks.

A wheat-free diet has much to commend it, and can be a great opportunity to change your life for the better. Even for those who can eat wheat, building wheat-free meals into your diet adds variety and gives your digestion a welcome break. This book shows you how simple it is to make everyday changes. It is divided into six chapters which are designed to make it easy to find the right recipe at the right time of day – whether you're looking for a tasty brunch bite, food for friends or for a treat. You will also find our wheat-free recipes familiar, and exactly the kind of food suited to modern tastes and lifestyles. We hope you will enjoy them.

Happy wheat-free eating!

Essential know-how

What is food intolerance?

Food intolerance is an inability to tolerate a particular food or foods. Put simply, it means the food doesn't suit you, and causes detrimental physical side-effects (see symptoms on page 11) and general malabsorption of foods. It may be mild or severe, and can happen at any stage in your life. Wheat and lactose intolerance are two of the most common food intolerances; other foods regularly cited include shellfish, citrus fruits and tree nuts such as Brazil nuts.

No one knows for sure what causes food intolerances. As far as wheat is concerned, many health specialists believe that the overdependence on wheat in our diet – eating too much bread, pasta and pizzas for example – and the fact that most of the wheat we eat is highly processed, are major contributing factors. In short, our diets are literally overloaded with wheat. The good news is that by excluding the offending food, the food intolerance can in time be reversed or significantly improved so that you can tolerate small amounts of it without any debilitating effects. An intolerance may also be transient and children, for example, may 'grow out of' their wheat allergy.

Food intolerance or food allergy?

Unlike food intolerance, where symptoms may take a few days to show themselves and may not be clear-cut, an allergic reaction is a specific immunological reaction and is usually immediate. Common allergic reactions include itchy skin, and swelling of the mouth and throat. (In extreme cases, this swelling can be severe and result in anaphylaxis.) A food allergy cannot be reversed, and will need to be properly diagnosed by your GP, or medically qualified allergy specialist. The only way to combat its effects is to completely exclude the offending food from your diet for life. It is estimated that in the UK up to 15% of the population report adverse food reactions, and that 1–4% of the general population and 6% of children suffer from food allergies.

Wheat intolerance or gluten intolerance?

Gluten intolerance is an inability to tolerate gluten, a protein found in wheat, rye and barley (it is also found in a lesser degree in oats, though research shows oats from uncontaminated sources may often be tolerated). It is a chronic lifelong, genetically linked medical condition, and it causes coeliac disease – inflammation of the intestinal lining of the small bowel or, more rarely, the skin rash dermatitis herpetiformis (DH). It affects all ages, including infants, and sufferers must practise strict avoidance of these grains and eat a gluten-free diet for life. The Coeliac Society estimates that 1% of the population are coeliacs. Unlike wheat intolerance, gluten intolerance is not reversible.

In reality, because the symptoms are so similar and the main sources of gluten are wheat and wheat products, it is often difficult to distinguish between gluten intolerance and wheat intolerance. There are many people who feel they are wheat intolerant who may actually be gluten intolerant. That is why, if you feel you may be suffering from a food intolerance, it is important to undergo a proper diagnosis with a properly qualified allergy specialist/gastroenterologist arranged by your GP.

Common symptoms of wheat intolerance

Many of the following symptoms are not exclusively to wheat intolerance, but if you regularly suffer from some of them with no obvious reason why, then wheat may be a cause. Like gluten intolerance, the symptoms may come and go.

▸ **Bloating** *
▸ **Flatulence**
▸ **Fatigue, lack of energy, and general tiredness** *
▸ **IBS (Irritable Bowel Syndrome)**
▸ **Headaches**
▸ **Constipation/diarrhoea**
▸ **Foggy thinking***
▸ **Feeling below par**
▸ **Lack of motivation, general negativity, depression**
▸ **Fluctuating weight**
▸ **Craving for wheat**

*Symptoms most commonly associated with wheat intolerance

How do I know if I am wheat intolerant?

The simplest way to assess whether you may be intolerant of wheat is to use the recipes in this book to help you exclude all wheat and wheat products from your diet, and to monitor any lessening of symptoms. You must be rigorous and will need to follow a wheat-free diet for around four weeks to give your body the chance to 'detoxify' properly. Seek medical advice if necessary first.

▸ **Keep a food diary for at least one week before you adopt your wheat-free diet, writing down what you eat, and any symptoms.**
▸ **While on your wheat-free diet, continue your diary and monitor symptoms.**
▸ **You may initially experience headaches, or feel worse when you first start your wheat-free regime. Don't worry: this is a common reaction to detoxification and it is temporary.**
▸ **At the end of four weeks, gradually reintroduce wheat into your diet: choose 100% wheat products – pasta, bread, and so on, and monitor your body's reaction, eating a little more of the food every day for at least three days. If you get a reaction, stop eating wheat.**

If your symptoms improve, and you have an adverse reaction when reintroducing wheat, seek medical advice to confirm your diagnosis and whether you are intolerant to wheat or gluten.

What next?

Learning more about food intolerances and how changing your diet can affect your health for the better, will help you enormously in planning your own wheat-free lifestyle. For where to start, see below.

Adapting to a wheat-free diet

Eating a wheat-free diet could not be simpler. Major supermarkets, health food stores, and organic shops stock a wide range of wheat-free products, including breakfast cereals, flours, breads, pasta, cakes and biscuits. Supermarkets also produce lists of their own-label wheat-free products. Expert advice and help, as well as sources of wheat- and gluten-free products, are easy to find on the internet (see page 158), wheat-free cookery courses are common, and because many people today are wheat intolerant, or prefer not to include wheat in their diet, you – and your children – should have little difficulty in eating out, and no need to feel awkward at parties and other social occasions. Adapting meals and recipes is also very easy – for how to, see page 17.

Getting started: which foods should I avoid?

It is important to learn which common foods contain wheat, and therefore should be eliminated from your diet. They are:

- ✗ All wheat flours and products derived from wheat: sprouted wheat grains, wheatgerm, wheat bran, semolina, bulgur, couscous.
- ✗ All breads, pizzas, pastas and noodles containing wheat flour.
- ✗ All muesli that contains wheat flakes or bran flakes; breakfast cereals containing wheat or wheat bran for example Shredded Wheat, Weetabix, Bran Flakes.
- ✗ All pastry including filo pastry, cakes, biscuits, crackers and pretzels, except those which specifically state that they are wheat-free on the label.
- ✗ Pancakes, tortillas, pittas, chappatis, naan bread, poppadoms.
- ✗ All sausages, except 100% meat sausages, and those that specifically state that they are wheat- or gluten-free on the label.
- ✗ All foods coated in breadcrumbs (such as fish fingers and fishcakes); stuffings containing breadcrumbs, and gratins with bread toppings.
- ✗ All foods coated in batter, such as traditional fried fish and Japanese tempura.
- ✗ Sauces, soups, desserts, condiments, confectionery and snacks containing flour or wheat starch.
- ✗ Soy (shoyu) sauce and miso made from wheat.
- ✗ Beers and lagers, where wheat is used in the brewing process.

Which foods can I eat?

A wheat-free diet is a wonderful opportunity to discover many delicious foods that you may not have included in your diet previously, so far from feeling deprived, many people find that a wheat-free diet is a very rewarding and exciting way to eat. The list of foods you can enjoy is as varied as you want to make it. These are the foods you can safely eat on a wheat-free diet.

- ✓ Dairy products.
- ✓ Fish.
- ✓ Meat.
- ✓ Vegetables, salads and fruit.
- ✓ Tofu products.
- ✓ Dried beans and pulses.
- ✓ Nuts and seeds.
- ✓ Dried fruits.

✓ Herbs and spices.

✓ Quorn.

✓ Grains: rice (all varieties) barley, millet, amaranth, quinoa, buckwheat, sago, sorghum, tapioca.

✓ All products made from maize (corn): tortilla chips, tacos, polenta, corn breads, corn crispbreads, popcorn.

✓ All products made from oats: porridge, flapjacks, oat biscuits, oatmeal, oatbran.

✓ All products made from chickpea (gram) flour e.g. falafel, onion bhajis.

✓ Rice cakes, rice noodles.

✓ Buckwheat pancakes and Japanese (100% soba) noodles; Asian glass noodles (made from pea and bean flour).

✓ Flour: oat, barley, maize, gram, soya, sago, tapioca, rice, arrowroot, potato, cornflour.

✓ All prepared foods that specifically state that they are wheat-free on the label.

Which breads can I eat?

✓ 100% rye breads, crispbreads and crackers.

✓ German pumpernickel and wheat-free grain breads.

✓ Home-made wheat-free breads.

✓ All manufactured breads that specifically state that they are wheat-free on the label.

✓ Gluten-free breads are usually wheat-free also.

Note: Many gluten-free breads are expensive and white breads in particular can contain a wide range of processing aids and ingredients. Choose natural rye bread, wheat-free wholegrain breads, or home-made gluten-free breads as your everyday bread. When buying breads, choose organic breads when you can.

What about spelt and kamut?

These are little-known but very nutritious varieties of wheat. People who are sensitive to common bread wheat, *Triticum vulgare*, or who have wheat intolerance (as opposed to the more serious wheat allergy) often find that they can eat spelt and kamut. Spelt and kamut breads, pastas and breakfast cereals are all available.

Note: Because spelt and kamut contain gluten, they are not suitable for gluten-free diets, and must be avoided by coeliacs and people with gluten intolerance.

What about processed food and ready-prepared meals?

This is a much more difficult area, primarily because common processing aids, particularly thickeners and fillers, are often wheat based and can be found hidden in the most unlikely foods and ingredients – for example, yogurts, mustard powder and spice mixtures, mayonnaise, stock cubes, sauces and condiments, including tomato sauce, as well as meat products such as sausages, meat patties, and cooked meats. As a general rule, keep processed foods and ready-prepared foods to a minimum. For preference, also choose brands that specialize in wheat-free products. If your intolerance is severe, only buy those products that state that they are wheat-free on the label.

Tips

▶ Read all labels very carefully: look for 'wheat-free'.
▶ Avoid foods that have rusk, modified starch (or corn), wheat starch, hydrolized wheat protein, wheat gluten, or raising agents containing wheat starch on the ingredients list.
▶ Organic wheat-free products will have fewer processing aids.
▶ If in any doubt, choose another product or make your own!

What about gluten-free products?

Generally, foods that are gluten-free are safe for wheat-free diets. However, gluten-free products may also contain wheat starch or other wheat proteins which, depending on the severity of the wheat intolerance, may cause aggravation. Check labels very carefully, and to be absolutely sure, choose products that state that they are wheat-free as well as gluten-free.

Top Tips for successful wheat-free eating

▶ Build your diet around fresh foods that are wheat-free. Eat regular meals.
▶ Plan ahead: take fruit, a ripe avocado, wheat-free nut and seed bars, and healthy wheat-free snacks such as falafels with you to snack on when you go out.
▶ For a packed lunch, try salad, hummus or other dips and crudité, or wholegrain wheat-free sandwiches, or take a flask of soup.
▶ When eating out, check that the dishes you have chosen do not contain hidden wheat.
▶ Don't think deprivation, think liberation!

In the kitchen

Cooking wheat-free food generally requires minimal changes in the kitchen. In fact, the only area where you will notice any significant difference is baking, but even here most recipes can be adapted very easily.

Wheat-free pastas

All gluten-free pastas are suitable for wheat-free diets, and there is a wide range to choose from, all varying slightly in taste, depending on the flour they are made from. The main difference between wheat-free and wheat pasta is that wheat-free pasta becomes too soft very quickly, so you need to watch cooking times very closely, and drain the pasta immediately after cooking.

Easy substitutions

If you're worried about what to use instead of wheat, look no further than the table below to find out what to substitute in its place. You don't need to miss out on favourites like pasta and pizza just plan ahead and learn a few simple rules.

Wheat-free baking

Wheat-free flours often have a different texture to wheat flour and take a bit of getting used to, but make very good substitutes. Some, for example maize, chestnut, buckwheat and gram (chickpea), have distinct flavours. Others, like rice and tapioca flours, are bland. They are usually not suitable used on their own. Experiment to find which blend/combination works best for you.

▸ **Wheat-free flours tend to absorb more liquid. Be prepared to add a little extra liquid to achieve the right consistency for the recipe.**

▸ **Gluten-free flours, available from supermarkets and health food shops, are usually suitable for wheat-free diets and can be substituted for wheat flour when making pastry, and baking cakes and biscuits.**

▸ **Spelt flour (if you can tolerate it) can be substituted for brown and wholewheat flours.**

▸ **When using proprietary gluten-free flours, allow 1 tsp of wheat-free baking powder per 225g (8oz) flour when making cakes.**

▸ **Adding ground almonds, 25–50g (1–2oz), as part of the quantity of wheat-free flour required in a cake mix adds a delicious touch of luxury to home-made cakes and helps keep the cake moist.**

▸ **Maize (polenta) makes nutty, grainy cakes: use all polenta, or a mixture of**

Regular food	Wheat-free substitute
Pasta	Wheat-free pastas can be used for all recipes.
Pizza base	Ready-made gluten-free base, or make your own using gluten-free flour.
Wraps and pancakes	Buckwheat pancakes (see page 31) solve all your problems. Or try rice pancakes, substituting ground brown/white rice flour for wheat flour in your usual recipe.
Couscous and bulgur	Quinoa. It is more nutritious, easy to cook and delicious. Use it for all couscous and bulgur recipes. A great choice, too, for pilafs and salads.
Breadcrumbs	Maize (polenta) gives a delicious crispy coating to foods such as fishcakes and fried chicken.
Flour	Use rice flour for lining cake and bread tins; use gluten-free flour for dusting meat and fish.
Crumbles	Oatmeal or oatflakes, or a mixture of oatmeal and ground nuts makes a nutritious crumble topping.
Sandwiches	Rye breads, and German-style wheat-free grain breads make sandwiches packed with good carbs.
Snacks	Rice cakes and corn and rye crispbreads are perfect.

polenta and gluten-free flour, or a mixture of polenta, ground nuts and gluten-free flour.

▸ Chestnut flour (up to 10%) adds a deep richness to cakes; soya flour (up to 5%) makes a cake more nutritious. Both have strong flavours, so use small amounts.

▸ A mixture of brown rice flour and tapioca flour makes good biscuits.

▸ Substituting gluten-free flour with rice flour for half the quantity of flour required adds texture to cakes and biscuits.

▸ Try using half rice flour and half buckwheat flour in your Christmas cake or rich fruit cakes. Rye flour also produces good results.

▸ Corn breads are ideal for brunch. Use all maize flour or a mixture of maize flour and gram (chickpea) flour. Add extra flavours or a little sugar to mask maize flour's inherent bitterness.

▸ Gram (chickpea) flour makes extra-savoury cheese biscuits. Use up to 10%. A little chickpea flour can also be added to pastry mixes, and helps keep the pastry firm.

- Try making your own oatcakes – it is easy to do.
- Ground almonds/walnuts/hazelnuts make delicious macaroons.

Thickeners

Arrowroot, cornflour, potato flour and wheat-free thickening granules made from potato flour, available in supermarkets, can be used instead of flour to thicken savoury and sweet dishes. Unlike wheat flour, they are usually mixed in a little water (slaked) before adding to the dish. Follow the instructions on the packet.

Choosing the best

Changing to a wheat-free diet unlocks your taste buds and gives you an appetite for, and appreciation of, fresh, flavourful food. Seek out local produce and an organic vegetable box scheme, shop at farmers' markets and choose free-range and organic foods. This will instantly make your food taste better and is a great way to eat healthily and add variety to your diet.

Storecupboard

If you are allergic to wheat you must ensure that all spices, spice pastes, sweet and savoury bottled sauces, condiments, soy sauce and miso, canned goods, beers and lager are wheat-free. Read the labels carefully to check. It is a good idea to choose brands that do not contain wheat fillers or thickeners.

10 steps to health

Changing to a wheat-free diet will help you feel better and healthier. Incorporating your new, wheat-free way of eating into a healthy lifestyle, by following the simple steps below, will literally set you up for life and ensure you achieve maximum health and vitality.

1. Water

Water is the elixir of life and is nature's prime detoxifier. Aim to drink at least 1 litre ($1^{3}/_{4}$ pints) per day, or preferably 1–2 litres ($1^{3}/_{4}$ – $3^{1}/_{2}$ pints).

2. Vegetables, salads and fruit

Make sure your diet contains plenty of these. Not only are they a storehouse of vitamins and minerals but they help balance acidic foods such as dairy products and proteins, thus keeping the body at its optimum pH, which is slightly alkaline.

3. Superfood good carbs

Make sure your diet contains plenty of complex, unrefined, good carbohydrates such as whole grains, pulses and nuts and seeds. These are low-GI foods which will sustain your energy levels and help maintain your ideal weight.

4. Superfood good fats

Fats are essential to all life processes and a low-fat diet is not a good idea for long-term health. The trick is to replace bad fats (saturated fats and hydrogenated vegetable oil) with omega-rich unsaturated fats, which are found in certain vegetable oils. Nuts, seeds and oily fish are also good sources of these.

5. Eat regularly

Skipping meals leads to energy dips, stresses your system and is a sure-fire way to put on weight. Eating regularly keeps your physical and mental energy levels steady, preventing hunger pangs and the desire to snack.

6. Avoid processed foods

Most processed foods contain hidden wheat or gluten in the form of modified starch, so it is vital for anyone allergic to wheat or gluten to avoid them. Generally, too, the more your diet contains fresh, unprocessed 'real' foods, the better it is for your health.

7. Variety

Enjoy as wide a variety of foods as possible. This way you will ensure that your diet contains all the health-giving micro-nutrients it needs for optimum health. It also lessens the likelihood of developing food intolerances to particular foods.

8. Exercise regularly

Exercise is vital. It energises you, raises your metabolic rate, helps you to maintain your correct weight, reduces stress and helps you sleep better.

9. Stress less

Stress comes in all shapes and sizes, whether it is pressure at work, noise, traffic or the constant barrage of environmental and electronic pollution. Reduce stress by learning some simple deep-breathing techniques.

10. Sleep

Sleep is Nature's happy pill, the ultimate physical and mental reviver, and the secret to staying young. Make getting enough sleep a top priority.

Start the day

Starting the day with a good breakfast is one of the cornerstones of healthy eating. If you usually skimp or miss breakfast, now is the time to change. Research shows that it is the most important meal of the day. People who miss breakfast suffer more energy dips and loss of concentration, and are more likely to have weight-control problems. Turn the page and take your pick from instant nutrient-rich breakfasts to lazy brunches.

Raspberry and kiwi smoothie

Serves 2

Hands-on time: 8 minutes

Cooking time: none

110 cals, 0g fat, 24g carbohydrate per serving

3 kiwi fruit

200g (7oz) raspberries

200–250ml (7–9fl oz) freshly-squeezed orange juice

4 tbsp Greek-style yogurt

1 Peel and roughly chop the kiwi fruit and put into a blender with the raspberries, orange juice and yogurt. Blend until smooth, then serve.

Mango and organic oat smoothie

Serves 2

Hands-on time: 8 minutes

Cooking time: none

200 cals, 2g fat (of which 1g saturates), 41g carbohydrate per serving

150g (5oz) natural yogurt

1 small mango, peeled, stoned and chopped

2 tbsp organic oats

4 ice cubes

1 Put the yogurt into a blender. Add the chopped mango, oats and ice cubes and blend until smooth. Serve immediately.

Energy-boosting muesli

Makes 15 servings

Hands-on time: 10 minutes

Cooking time: none

210 cals, 8g fat (of which 1g saturates), 28g carbohydrate per serving

500g (1lb 2oz) organic porridge oats

100g (3^1/$_2$oz) toasted almonds, chopped

2 tbsp each pumpkin and sunflower seeds

100g (3^1/$_2$oz) ready-to-eat dried apricots, chopped

1 Mix together the oats, almonds, seeds and apricots.

2 Store in a sealable container for up to one month.

▼ **COOK'S TIP**

Oats contain gluten and, strictly speaking, are not suitable for coeliacs. However, because they contain much smaller amounts than wheat, rye or barley, research shows that most people with coeliac disease can safely eat moderate amounts. The oats must be from sources where there is no risk of contamination from wheat or wheat products during processing or packing. As individual tolerances to gluten vary, if you are a coeliac, seek expert advice before eating oats.

Toasted organic oats with berries

Serves 4

Hands-on time: 10 minutes

Cooking time: 5–10 minutes

260 cals, 8g fat (of which 1g saturates), 37g carbohydrate per serving

25g (1oz) hazelnuts

125g (4oz) organic oats

1 tbsp olive oil

125g (4oz) strawberries

250g (9oz) blueberries

200g (5oz) Greek-style yogurt

2 tbsp runny honey

1 Preheat the grill to medium. Roughly chop the hazelnuts and put into a bowl with the oats. Drizzle with the olive oil, mix well, then spread out on a baking sheet. Toast the oat mixture for 5–10 minutes until it starts to crisp up. Remove from the heat and set aside to cool.

2 Slice the strawberries and put into a large bowl with the blueberries and yogurt. Stir in the oats and hazelnuts, drizzle with the honey and divide among four dishes. Serve immediately.

Quick compôte

Serves 2

Hands-on time: 10 minutes

Cooking time: 5 minutes

170 cals, 7g fat (of which 1g saturates), 26g carbohydrate per serving

250g (9oz) cooking apples, peeled and chopped

Juice of $1/2$ organic lemon

1 tbsp golden caster sugar

Ground cinnamon

to serve

25g (1oz) raisins

25g (1oz) chopped almonds

1 tbsp natural yogurt

1 Put the cooking apples into a pan with the lemon juice, caster sugar and 2 tbsp cold water. Cook gently for 5 minutes until soft.

2 Sprinkle a little ground cinnamon over the top and chill. It will keep for up to three days.

3 Serve with the raisins, chopped almonds and yogurt.

▼ **COOK'S TIP**

Put the apples, lemon, sugar and water into a microwave-safe bowl, cover loosely with clingfilm and cook on high in a 850W microwave for 5 minutes until the apple is just soft.

Seeded wheat-free loaf

Makes 16 slices

Hands-on time: 15 minutes, plus rising time

Cooking time: 45–50 minutes, plus cooling time

140 cals, 2g fat (of which trace saturates), 26g carbohydrate per slice

2 tsp easy-blend dried yeast

2 tsp light muscovado sugar

Vegetable oil, to oil

300g (11oz) gluten-free white bread flour, plus

   extra to dust

200g (7oz) gluten-free brown bread flour

1 tbs each sunflower, linseed and poppy seeds

1 tsp salt

1 medium egg, lightly beaten

1 Stir the yeast and sugar into 150ml ($^1/_4$ pint) tepid water and leave to stand for 15 minutes until frothy. Lightly oil a 900g (2lb) loaf tin.

2 In a large bowl, beat together the flour, seeds, salt, yeast mixture, egg and a further 250ml (8fl oz) tepid water to make a soft, thick pastey dough. Form into an oblong shape on a lightly floured surface and drop into the loaf tin. Cover with lightly oiled clingfilm and leave to rise in a warm place for 45 minutes or until it reaches the top of the tin. Slash the top with a sharp knife and dust with flour.

3 Bake at 200°C (180°C fan oven) mark 6 for 45–50 minutes or until the loaf sounds hollow when tapped underneath. Transfer to a wire rack and leave to cool.

▼ COOK'S TIP

Gluten-free breads are more cake-like in texture and taste but are still suitable for all recipes requiring bread. If you have a bread making machine, use this, following the manufacturer's instructions.

Breakfast bruschetta

Serves 4

Hands-on time: 5 minutes

Cooking time: none

170 cals, 1g fat (of which 0g saturates), 32g carbohydrate per serving

1 ripe banana

250g (9oz) blueberries

200g (7oz) Quark

1 tbsp runny honey

4 slices pumpernickel or wheat-free
  wholegrain bread

1 Slice the banana and put in a bowl with the blueberries.

2 Spoon in the Quark and mix well.

3 Toast the slices of bread on both sides, then spread with the blueberry mixture.

4 Drizzle with the honey and serve immediately.

▼ COOK'S TIP

Blueberries are delicious and an excellent fruit for healthy breakfasts. Recent research shows that blueberries are one of the best sources of antioxidants. They may even help to protect against ageing and ageing diseases, and to reduce high cholesterol levels. They also help to keep the gut and urinary tract healthy.

Spiced apricot yogurt

Serves 1
Hands-on time: 8 minutes
Cooking time: none
180 cals, 1g fat (of which trace saturates), 36g carbohydrate per serving

1 ball stem ginger, chopped

1 tsp ginger syrup (from the stem ginger jar)

150g (5oz) natural yogurt

1 ripe apricot, stoned and chopped

1 Stir the chopped stem ginger and the ginger syrup into the yogurt, together with the chopped apricot.

Organic oats with apple juice

Serves 6–8
Hands-on time: 5 minutes, plus chilling time
Cooking time: none
170–130 cals, 0g fat, 34–26g carbohydrate per serving

200g (7oz) organic oats

500ml (16fl oz) apple juice

1 Put the oats into a large bowl and pour the apple juice over them.

2 Cover and chill overnight. Serve with yogurt or fresh fruit salad.

Sunday brunch buckwheat pancakes

Makes 4

Hands-on time: 5 minutes

Cooking time: 15 minutes

160 cals, 4g fat (of which 1g saturates), 27g carbohydrate per pancake

125g (4oz) wheat-free buckwheat pancake mix

1 medium egg

About 125ml (4fl oz) milk and water mixed

A little oil, to fry

1 Put the flour into a bowl and make a well in the centre. Break the egg into the well and add a little of the milk and water. Mix the liquid ingredients together, then gradually beat in the flour until smooth.

2 Beat in the remaining milk; the batter should be the consistency of double cream (alternatively, use the blender). Add a dash more milk if necessary.

3 Heat a pancake pan. When hot, brush with a minimum of oil. Add a little extra milk to the batter if it is too thick. Spoon a quarter of the batter into the pan and swirl it around until it is evenly spread over the bottom of the pan.

4 Cook over a low to medium-high heat for about 2 minutes or until the edges are cooked and bubbles appear on the surface. Flip the pancake over using a palette knife and cook for 1 minute or so until the underside is browned.

5 Turn the pancake out on to a sheet of greaseproof paper. Keep warm and repeat until all the pancake batter has been used, lightly oiling the pan in between and stacking the pancakes as they are cooked. To serve, spread with fruit compôte and thick yogurt. Alternatively, fill with cooked apple slices or cooked apple and blackberries.

Blueberry muffins

Makes 12

Hands-on time: 15 minutes

Cooking time: 15 minutes, plus cooling time

220 cals, 8g fat (of which 3g saturates), 36g carbohydrate per serving

250g (9oz) wheat-free flour

2 level tsp wheat-free baking powder

1 tsp bicarbonate of soda

125g (4oz) golden caster sugar

75g (3oz) ground almonds

Finely grated zest of 1 organic lemon

125g (4oz) dried blueberries

1 medium egg

1 tsp vanilla extract

250ml (9fl oz) skimmed milk

50g (2oz) unsalted butter, melted

1 Preheat the oven to 200°C (180°C fan oven) mark 6. Line a muffin tin with 12 paper muffin cases.

2 Put the flour, baking powder and bicarbonate of soda into a bowl, then stir in the caster sugar, ground almonds, lemon zest and dried blueberries.

3 Put the egg, vanilla extract, milk and butter into a jug and mix together with a fork. Pour this liquid into the dry ingredients and lightly fold together.

4 Spoon the mixture into the muffin cases to three-quarters full and bake in the oven for 15 minutes or until the muffins are risen, pale golden and just firm.

5 Transfer the muffins to a wire rack and leave to cool slightly. Dust with icing sugar to serve.

Classic French omelette

Serves 1

Hands-on time: 5 minutes

Cooking time: about 2 minutes

360–450 cals, 34–40g fat (of which 17–19g saturates),
0g carbohydrate per serving

2–3 medium eggs

1 tbsp milk or water

25g (1oz) unsalted butter, to fry

1 Whisk the eggs in a bowl – just enough to break them down; over-beating spoils the texture of the omelette. Season with salt and pepper and add the milk or water.

2 Heat the butter in an 18cm (7in) omelette pan or non-stick frying pan until it is foaming, but not brown.

3 Add the beaten eggs and stir gently with a fork or wooden spatula, drawing the mixture from the sides to the centre as it sets and letting the liquid egg in the centre run to the sides. When set, stop stirring and cook for a further 30 seconds or until the omelette is golden brown underneath and still creamy on top; don't overcook.

4 If you are making a filled omelette (see below), add the filling at this point.

5 Tilt the pan away from you slightly and use a palette knife to fold over one-third of the omelette to the centre, then fold over the opposite third. Slide the omelette out on to a warmed plate, letting it flip over so that the folded sides are underneath. Serve immediately, with sliced or grilled tomatoes.

▼ VARIATION

- Blend 25g (1oz) mild goat's cheese and blend with 1 tbsp crème fraîche; put in the centre of the omelette before folding.

- Toss 25g (1oz) chopped smoked salmon or cooked smoked haddock with a little chopped dill and 1 tbs crème fraîche; scatter over the omelette before folding.

Brunch hash browns

Serves 4–6

Hands-on time: 15 minutes

Cooking time: 35 minutes

**310-200 cals, 14-9g fat (of which 7-5g saturates),
42-28g carbohydrate per serving**

700g (1lb 8oz) medium potatoes (unpeeled)

50g (2oz) butter

1 small onion, chopped

2 red onions, cut into rings

Sunflower oil, to brush

450g (1lb) small vine-ripened tomatoes

1 Add the potatoes to a pan of salted cold water, bring to the boil and parboil for 10 minutes. Drain, then cut into 2.5cm (1in) cubes.

2 Heat the butter in a large frying pan with a heavy base, add the chopped onion and fry for 1 minute. Add the potatoes and fry over a medium heat for 25 minutes or until crisp and brown, turning frequently.

3 Halfway through cooking, preheat the grill to medium-high. Brush the onion rings with oil and add to the grill pan with the tomatoes. Grill for about 10 minutes until softened and lightly caramelized. Serve with fried eggs or lean roast ham.

4 Serve the hash browns with the onion rings and tomatoes. Good to accompany with fried eggs or lean roast ham.

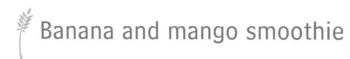

Banana and mango smoothie

Serves 2. Makes about 600ml (1 pint)
Hands-on time: 5 minutes plus chilling time
Cooking time: none
270 cals, 34g fat (of which 0g saturates), 56g carbohydrate per serving

1 ripe mango, peeled and roughly chopped

1 banana, peeled

200ml (7fl oz) semi-skimmed milk

150–200ml (5–7fl oz) freshly squeezed orange juice

3 tbsp Greek-style yogurt

1 tbsp icing sugar (optional)

1 Put the mango in a blender or food processor with the remaining ingredients, then whiz for 1 minute or until smooth.

2 Chill well, then pour into glasses and serve.

Smoked haddock rarebit

Serves 4

Hands-on time: 5 minutes

Cooking time: 10-15 minutes

400 cals, 14g fat (of which 8g saturates), 24g carbohydrate per serving

4 x 150g (5oz) smoked haddock fillets, skinned

4 slices gluten-free bread

200g (7oz) spinach

300g (11oz) low-fat créme fraîche

2 large tomatoes

1 Preheat the grill. Season the haddock fillets and put into a shallow ovenproof dish. Grill for 6–8 minutes until opaque and cooked through.

2 Toast the bread on both sides until golden.

3 Wash the spinach, squeeze out the water and put in a pan. Cover and cook for 1-2 minutes until starting to wilt. Tip into a bowl. Slice the tomatoes.

4 Top each piece of bread with a piece of fish, then add the spinach and tomato slices. Spoon over the créme fraîche it and grill for 2–3 minutes to heat through. Season with freshly ground black pepper and serve.

Rösti potatoes with fried eggs

Serves 4

Hands-on time: 20 minutes, plus cooling time

Cooking time: 35–40 minutes

330 cals, 16g fat (of which 7g saturates), 39g carbohydrate per serving

900g (2lb) red potatoes, scrubbed and left whole

40g (1¹⁄₂oz) butter

4 large eggs

1 Put the potatoes into a pan of cold water. Cover, bring to the boil and parboil for 5–8 minutes. Drain and leave to cool for 15 minutes.

2 Preheat the oven to 150°C (130°C fan oven) mark 2 and put a baking tray inside to warm. Peel the potatoes and coarsely grate them lengthways to give long strands. Divide into eight portions and shape into mounds.

3 Melt half the butter in a large, non-stick frying pan. Once it is bubbling and beginning to brown, put four of the potato mounds in the pan, spacing them well apart, and flatten them a little.

4 Fry slowly for about 6–7 minutes until golden brown, then turn them over and brown the second side for 6–7 minutes. Transfer the rösti to a warmed baking tray and keep warm in a low oven while you fry the rest.

5 Just before serving, carefully break the eggs into the hot pan and fry for about 2 minutes until the white is set and the yolk is still soft. Season with salt and pepper and serve at once, with the rösti.

Poached eggs with mushrooms and pesto

Serves 4

Hands-on time: 15 minutes

Cooking time: 20 minutes

300 cals, 24g fat (of which 10g saturates), 1g carbohydrate per serving

8 medium-sized flat or Portobello mushrooms

40g (1½oz) butter

8 medium eggs

225g (8oz) baby spinach leaves

4 tsp good-quality fresh pesto

1 Preheat the oven to 200°C (180°C fan oven) mark 6. Arrange the mushrooms in a single layer in a small roasting tin and dot with the butter. Roast for 15 minutes until golden brown and soft.

2 Meanwhile, bring a wide, shallow pan of water to the boil. When the mushrooms are half-cooked and the water is bubbling furiously, break the eggs into the pan, spaced well apart, then immediately take the pan off the heat. The eggs will take about 6 minutes to cook.

3 When the mushrooms are tender, put them on a warmed plate, cover and return to the turned-off oven to keep warm.

4 Put the roasting tin over a medium heat on the hob and add the spinach. Cook, stirring, for about 30 seconds until the spinach has just started to wilt.

5 The eggs should be set by now, so divide the mushrooms among four plates and top with a little spinach, a poached egg and a teaspoonful of pesto.

Quick bites

It is as important to eat well at lunchtime as it is at dinnertime. This does not mean cooking complicated meals; you don't even need to cook at all if you don't feel like it, or time is short. It simply means ensuring that you and your family enjoy some fresh, wholesome food.

Polenta with mixed mushrooms

Grilled sardines with harissa

Green beans and flaked almonds

Spicy popcorn

Chickpeas with spinach

Quick tuna salad

Smoked fish with hot horseradish

Grilled sardines

Salmon niçoise

Quick ginger, leek and prawn stir-fry

Special fried rice

Egg and pepper pizza

Tomato salsa

Purple sprouting broccoli with toasted pine nuts

Parmesan crisps

Courgette and parmesan frittata

Polenta with mixed mushrooms

Serves 8

Hands-on time: 10 minutes

Cooking time: 20 minutes

240 cals, 11g fat (of which 4g saturates), 29g carbohydrate per serving

50g (2oz) butter

1.1kg (2½lb) mixed mushrooms

1 red chilli (see page 74), deseeded and finely
   chopped

3 garlic cloves, peeled and sliced

100g (3½oz) sun-dried tomatoes, roughly chopped

1 tsp chopped thyme, plus thyme sprigs to garnish

1kg (2¼lb) ready-made polenta

3 tbsp olive oil

Truffle oil (optional)

1 Melt half the butter in a deep-sided frying pan or wok. Add half the mushrooms
and cook over a high heat until all the liquid has evaporated, then set aside. Repeat
with the remaining butter and mushrooms. Add the chilli and garlic to the pan and
fry for 2 minutes, then add to the mushrooms, together with the sun-dried tomatoes
and thyme. Mix well and season with salt and pepper.

2 Slice the polenta into 16 pieces, about 1cm (½in) thick. Heat the olive oil in a
non-stick frying pan. Add the polenta in batches, and fry for 3–4 minutes on each
side or until golden.

3 To serve, arrange two slices of polenta per person on a plate, top with the
mushroom sauce and drizzle with a little truffle oil, if using. Garnish with thyme
sprigs.

Grilled sardines with harissa

Serves 4 as a starter, 2 as a main course

Hands-on time: 10 minutes

Cooking time: 5–10 minutes

250 cals, 17g fat (of which 4g saturates), 0g carbohydrate

1 garlic clove, peeled and crushed

2 tbsp olive oil

1–2 tsp harissa

4 whole sardines

1 Preheat the grill to high. Put the garlic in a bowl. Add the oil and harissa, season to taste with salt and pepper, and mix together.

2 Slash the sardines a couple of times on each side, then brush the harissa and oil mixture all over. Grill for 5–10 minutes on each side until cooked through. Serve with grilled polenta and salad.

3 Serve with a green salad, tomato salad or watercress leaves as a starter, or with grilled polenta or boiled potatoes and broccoli with toasted pine nuts (see page 56) as a main course.

▼ **COOK'S TIP**

Oily fish like sardines are one of the best sources of essential heart-protecting omega 3 oils. Eat them at least once a week. Fresh Cornish sardines are a treat and are cheap. Look out for them at your fishmongers or on the fresh fish counter at the supermarket.

Green beans and flaked almonds

Serves 4

Hands-on time: 8 minutes

Cooking time: 15–20 minutes

60 cals, 5g fat (of which trace saturates), 2g carbohydrate per serving

200g (7oz) green beans

1 tsp olive oil

25g (1oz) flaked almonds

A little lemon juice

1 Bring a large pan of water to the boil. Add the green beans for 4–5 minutes. Drain.

2 Meanwhile, heat the oil in a large frying pan. Add the almonds and cook for 1–2 minutes until golden. Turn off the heat, add the drained beans to the frying pan and toss. Squeeze over a little lemon juice just before serving. Serve with grilled tuna.

Spicy popcorn

Serves 4

Hands-on time: 5 minutes

Cooking time: 10 minutes

150 cals, 11g fat (of which trace saturates), 12g carbohydrate per serving

100g (3¹/₂oz) popcorn

Pinch each of chilli and crushed cumin seeds

1 Microwave the popcorn (follow the packet instuctions) and tip into a bowl while still hot. Add the chilli and cumin and toss well. Serve as a snack or part of a buffet.

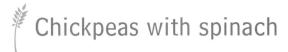

Chickpeas with spinach

Serves 6

Hands-on time: 10 minutes

Cooking time: about 15 minutes

190 cals, 10g fat (of which 1g saturates), 17g carbohydrate per serving

2.5cm (1in) piece fresh root ginger, peeled

3 garlic cloves, peeled

3 tbsp olive oil

2 tsp each ground coriander and paprika

1 tsp ground cumin

2 × 400g (14oz) chickpeas

4 tomatoes

Handful of coriander leaves

450g (1lb) spinach

1 Finely chop the ginger and chop the garlic. Heat the oil in a large pan with a heavy base, add the ginger, garlic and spices and cook for 2 minutes, stirring. Drain and rinse the chickpeas, then stir into the spices.

2 Roughly chop the tomatoes and add to the pan with the coriander leaves and spinach. Cook gently for 10 minutes. Season to taste with salt and pepper and serve immediately.

▼ **COOK'S TIP**

A good vegetarian dish. As a main course, serve with rice and a simple finely grated carrot salad tossed in a little lemon juice.

Quick tuna salad

Serves 2

Hands-on time: 10 minutes

Cooking time: none

300 cals, 8g fat (of which 1g saturates), 33g carbohydrate per serving

400g (14oz) canned mixed beans

125g (4oz) flaked tuna

$1/2$ cucumber, chopped

1 red onion, finely sliced

2 ripe tomatoes, chopped

2 celery sticks, chopped

Handful of baby spinach leaves

1 tbsp olive oil

2 tsp red wine vinegar

1 Drain the mixed beans, then tip into a bowl and add the flaked tuna, chopped cucumber, finely sliced red onion, chopped tomatoes, chopped celery and the spinach.

2 Mix together the oil and red wine vinegar, then toss through the bean mix. Serve.

▼ **COOK'S TIP**

A great low-GI meal and excellent packed lunch, which will sustain energy levels and ensure a slow release of blood sugars, helping to prevent hunger pangs and energy dips later on in the afternoon.

Smoked fish with hot horseradish

Serves 1
Hands-on time: 20 minutes
Cooking time: none
360 cals, 25g fat (of which 5g saturates), 13g carbohydrate per serving

Handful of cherry tomatoes, chopped

1/4 cucumber, sliced

2–3 celery sticks, sliced

1/2 head chicory, sliced

75g (3oz) flaked smoked trout or mackerel

100g (3 1/2 oz) natural yogurt

1 tsp hot horseradish sauce

1 Put the cherry tomatoes, cucumber, celery sticks and chicory into a shallow bowl. Add the flaked smoked trout and season with pepper.

2 In a small bowl, mix together the yogurt and horseradish sauce. Drizzle this over the salad and serve.

▼ **COOK'S TIP**

If you're on a dairy-free diet or are looking for an alternative to milk-based products, swap the yogurt for soya yogurt. Soya is a good source of essential omega-3 and omega-6 fatty acids, which help to lower cholesterol.

Grilled sardines

Serves 4

Hands-on time: 10 minutes

Cooking time: 4–5 minutes

220 cals, 8g fat (of which 2g saturates), 22g carbohydrate per serving

4 thick slices rye or wheat-free wholegrain bread

2 large tomatoes

2 x 125g (4oz) cans sardines in olive oil

Juice of $\frac{1}{2}$ organic lemon

Small handful of parsley

1 Preheat the grill. Toast the bread on both sides.

2 Meanwhile, slice the tomatoes and drain the sardines. Divide the tomatoes and the sardines among the toast slices, squeeze the lemon over them then put back under the grill for 2–3 minutes to heat through.

3 Snip the parsley, scatter on top and serve immediately.

▼ **COOK'S TIP**

For a piquant variation with chilli bite, try sardines picante (sardines canned with dried chillies) available in supermarkets.

Salmon niçoise

Serves 4

Hands-on time: 15 minutes

Cooking time: 10 minutes

270 cals, 18g fat (of which 4g saturates), 7g carbohydrate per serving

4 eggs

200g (7oz) cooked salmon flakes

400g (14oz) canned mixed beans, drained

50g (2oz) pitted black olives

250g (9oz) cherry tomatoes, halved

Large handful of mixed salad leaves

1 tbsp olive oil

Juice of $1/_2$ organic lemon

1 Cook the eggs in a pan of simmering water for 6 minutes. Drain, then peel and cut into quarters.

2 Put the eggs into a salad bowl with the salmon, mixed beans, olives, halved cherry tomatoes and a large handful of mixed salad leaves. Add the oil and lemon juice. Season with salt and pepper, toss together and serve.

Quick ginger, leek and prawn stir-fry

Serves 4

Hands-on time: 10 minutes

Cooking time: about 15 minutes

170 cals, 5g fat (of which 1g saturates), 6g carbohydrate per serving

2 tsp olive oil

1 bunch spring onions, chopped

1 garlic clove, peeled and crushed

2.5cm (1in) piece fresh root ginger, peeled
   and grated

3 leeks, roughly chopped

1 red pepper, halved, deseeded and roughly chopped

400g (14oz) cooked prawns

1 tbsp tamari sauce, (wheat-free Japanese
   soy sauce)

2 tsp tomato puree, diluted in 1 tbsp
   of water

1 tsp of runny honey

1 Heat the oil in a pan, add the spring onions, garlic, ginger and 2 tbsp water and fry for 2 minutes over a medium heat. Add the leeks and red pepper and stir-fry for 10 minutes until softened.

2 Add the prawns, tamari sauce, tomato paste and honey to the pan. Season with pepper and cook for 30 seconds to 1 minute, stirring. Serve with rice or quinoa.

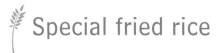

Special fried rice

Serves 4

Hands-on time: 5 minutes

Cooking time: about 20 minutes

350 cals, 13g fat (of which 2g saturates), 36g carbohydrate per serving

150g (5oz) American long-grain rice

2 tbsp sesame oil

3 eggs, lightly beaten

250g (9oz) frozen petits pois

250g (9oz) cooked ham, diced, or shredded chicken

1 Cook the rice according to the packet instructions. Drain well.

2 Heat 1 tsp oil in a large, non-stick frying pan. Pour in half the beaten eggs and tilt the pan around over the heat for about 1 minute until the egg is set. Tip the omelette on to a warmed plate. Repeat with 1 tsp oil and the remaining beaten egg to make another omelette. Tip on to another warmed plate.

3 Add the remaining oil to the pan and stir in the rice and peas. Stir-fry for 2–3 minutes until the peas are cooked. Add the ham or chicken.

4 Roll up the omelettes, roughly chop one-third of one, then slice the remainder into strips. Add the chopped omelette to the rice, peas and meat, then cook for 1–2 minutes to heat through. Divide among four bowls, top with the sliced omelette and eat immediately.

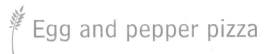

Egg and pepper pizza

Serves 4

Hands-on time: 5 minutes

Cooking time: 12 minutes

330 cals, 12g fat (of which 3g saturates), 40g carbohydrate per serving

150g (5oz) red and yellow marinated peppers in oil

8 tbsp passata

4 small wheat-free pizza bases

4 medium eggs

125g (4oz) watercress, washed and stalks removed

1 Preheat the oven to 220°C (200°C fan oven) mark 7. Preheat two large baking sheets, big enough to fit two pizzas each.

2 Drain the peppers, reserving the oil. Chop into thin strips. Spoon 2 tbsp passata over each pizza base and scatter strips of pepper around the edges. Make a dip in the passata in the middle of each pizza and break an egg into it. Carefully slide the pizzas on to the preheated baking sheets. Place in the oven and cook for 12 minutes until the egg is thoroughly cooked.

3 Top the pizzas with the watercress, drizzle with a little of the reserved oil from the peppers and serve.

▼ COOK'S TIP

Watercress is the salad superfood par excellence. It has been shown to have valuable anti-cancer and health-enhancing properties, and is a good source of iron, and vitamins C and E. Eat as often as you like. Add a few sprigs to salad leaves, and all kinds of salads and sandwiches, or to accompany grilled meat and all fish dishes. Finely chopped watercress can be stirred into soups, giving them a fresh, peppery tang.

Tomato salsa

Serves 4
Hands-on time: 15 minutes
Cooking time: none
160 cals, 15g fat (of which 2g saturates), 3g carbohydrate per serving

4 large ripe tomatoes

1 large ripe avocado

2 tbsp chopped coriander

Juice of 1 lime

2 tbsp olive oil

1 Cut the tomatoes into quarters and scoop out the seeds. Roughly chop the flesh and put into a bowl.

2 Slice the large avocado in half, remove the stone and scoop out the flesh with a spoon. Chop into pieces and add to the tomato with the chopped coriander.

3 Stir in the lime juice and oil. Serve with barbecued or grilled chicken or fish. Alternatively, spoon it over a green salad.

Purple sprouting broccoli with toasted pine nuts

Serves 8
Hands-on time: 5 minutes
Cooking time: about 10 minutes
110 cals, 7g fat (of which 1g saturates), 8g carbohydrate per serving

50g (2oz) pine nuts

1.1kg (2^1/$_2$lb) purple sprouting broccoli

50g (2oz) raisins

Small knob of butter

1 Put the pine nuts into a frying pan and dry-fry them for 2–3 minutes until golden. Set aside until needed.

2 Bring a large pan of water to the boil. Trim the ends off the broccoli and chop any large stems in two. Add to the water and cook for 3–4 minutes. Add the raisins and cook for a further 2–3 minutes or until the broccoli is tender.

3 Drain the broccoli and raisins well, then toss with the toasted pine nuts and butter. Serve at once with wheat-free pasta and shavings of Parmesan.

Parmesan crisps

Serves 8
Hands-on time: 5 minutes
Cooking time: about 10 minutes
110 cals, 7g fat (of which 1g saturates), 8g carbohydrate per serving

125g (4oz) freshly grated Parmesan cheese

^{1}/$_2$ tsp poppy seeds

1 Preheat the oven to 200°C (180°C fan oven) mark 6 and line two baking sheets with baking parchment. Evenly space heaped tablespoons of Parmesan on the sheets and spread each one out slightly. Sprinkle with poppy seeds and bake for 5–10 minutes until lacy and golden.

2 Leave on the tray for 2–3 minutes to cool and firm up slightly, then transfer to a wire rack. Serve as cocktail nibbles or to garnish soups (see page 70).

Courgette and parmesan frittata

Serves 4

Hands-on time: 10 minutes

Cooking time: 12 minutes

260 cals, 20g fat (of which 10g saturates), 4g carbohydrate per serving

40g (1$\frac{1}{2}$oz) butter

1 small onion, peeled and finely chopped

225g (8oz) courgettes, trimmed and finely sliced

6 medium eggs, beaten

25g (1oz) Parmesan cheese, freshly grated, plus

   shavings to garnish

1 Melt 25g (1oz) butter in an 18cm (7in) non-stick frying pan and cook the onion for about 10 minutes until softened. Add the courgettes and fry gently for 5 minutes or until they begin to soften.

2 Beat the eggs in a bowl and season with salt and pepper.

3 Add the remaining butter to the pan and heat, then pour in the eggs. Cook for 2–3 minutes or until golden underneath and cooked around the edges. Meanwhile, preheat the grill to medium.

4 Sprinkle the grated cheese over the frittata and grill for 1–2 minutes or until just set. Scatter with Parmesan shavings, cut into quarters and serve with a green salad.

▼ VARIATION

Cherry tomato and rocket frittata: replace the courgettes with 175g (6oz) ripe cherry tomatoes, frying them for 1 minute only, until they begin to soften. Immediately after pouring in the eggs, scatter 25g (1oz) rocket leaves over the surface. Continue as in main recipe.

Soups and salads

These recipes are designed for those in-between times when you don't want to cook a full meal but need something simple, healthy and nourishing. These dishes may be eaten at lunchtime or in the evening, depending on your timetable. Just use the freshest ingredients you can find to make them taste most delicious.

Thai spinach soup

Beetroot soup

Chicken broth

Squash and sweet potato soup

Special roasted tomato and pepper soup

Cucumber, yogurt and mint soup

Creamy watercress soup

Easy chicken salad

Green and orange salad

Roasted tomato salad

Classic coleslaw

Griddled polenta with Gorgonzola salad

Quinoa with mint dressing

Warm lentil, chicken and broccoli salad

Pasta salad with sun-dried tomatoes

Japanese noodle salad

Mild spiced chicken and quinoa

Thai spinach soup

Serves 4

Hands-on time: 15 minutes

Cooking time: 20–25 minutes

170 cals, 11g fat (of which 1g saturates), 4g carbohydrate per serving

2 tsp olive oil

1 tsp Thai green curry paste

1 bunch spring onions, thinly sliced

450g (1lb) fresh spinach, roughly chopped

200ml (7fl oz) low-fat coconut milk

600ml (1 pint) hot vegetable or chicken stock

1 Heat the oil and curry paste in a large pan. Add the spring onions and cook over a low heat, stirring, for 5–7 minutes.

2 Add the spinach and continue to cook until it begins to wilt.

3 Add the coconut milk and stock. Bring to the boil, then reduce the heat and simmer for 10–15 minutes. Leave to cool slightly.

4 Pour the mixture into a blender and whiz until smooth. Serve immediately.

Beetroot soup

Makes 2.4 litres (4^1/$_4$ pints) to serve 4 (and freeze for 4)

Hands-on time: 15 minutes

Cooking time: 40–45 minutes

150 cals, 7g fat (of which 3g saturates), 19g carbohydrate per serving

1 tbsp olive oil

1 onion, peeled and finely chopped

750g (1lb 10oz) raw beetroot, peeled and cut
   into 1cm (^{1}/$_2$ in) cubes

275g (10oz) potatoes, roughly chopped

2 litres (3^1/$_2$ pints) hot vegetable stock

Juice of 1 organic lemon

4 tbsp soured cream

25g (1oz) mixed root vegetable crisps

2 tbsp chopped chives, to garnish

1 Heat the oil in a large pan, add the onion and cook for 5 minutes. Add the vegetables and cook for a further 5 minutes.

2 Add the stock and lemon juice, then bring to the boil. Season with salt and pepper, reduce the heat and simmer, half-covered, for 25 minutes. Cool slightly, then whiz in a liquidizer until smooth.

3 Cool half the soup, then freeze it in a sealed container. It will keep for up to three months (defrost in the fridge overnight). Pour the remainder into a clean pan and reheat gently. Divide the soup among four warmed bowls. Add 1 tbsp soured cream to each bowl, top with a few vegetable crisps and sprinkle the chopped chives on top of the soup to serve.

4 Divide the soup between 4 warm bowls.

Chicken broth

Serves 4

Hands-on time: 30 minutes

Cooking time: about 15 minutes

230 cals, 8g fat (of which 2g saturates), 16g carbohydrate per serving

1 tbsp olive oil

About 300g (11oz) boneless, skinless chicken

   thighs, cubed

3 garlic cloves, peeled and crushed

2 medium red chillies, deseeded and finely diced

1 litre (1^3/$_4$ pints) chicken stock

50g (2oz) wheat-free pasta shapes or spaghetti,

   broken into short lengths

250g (9oz) each French beans, broccoli, sugar snap

   peas and courgettes, chopped

1 Heat the oil in a large pan, add the chicken, garlic and chilli (see page 74) and cook for 5–10 minutes or until the chicken is opaque all over.

2 Add the stock, bring to the boil, then add the vegetables and simmer for 5 minutes or until the chicken is cooked through.

3 Meanwhile, cook the pasta in a separate pan of salted boiling water until just cooked – about 5–10 minutes, depending on the type and thickness of the pasta.

4 Drain the pasta, add to the broth, and serve immediately.

Squash and sweet potato soup

Serves 8

Hands-on time: 15 minutes

Cooking time: 25 minutes

100 cals, 2g fat (of which trace saturates), 19g carbohydrate per serving

1 tbsp olive oil

1 large onion, peeled and finely chopped

1–2 medium red chillies (see page 74), deseeded
and chopped

2 tsp coriander seeds, crushed

1 butternut squash, about 750g (1lb 10oz), peeled,

deseeded and roughly chopped

2 medium sweet potatoes, peeled and

roughly chopped

2 tomatoes, skinned and diced

1.7 litres (3 pints) hot vegetable stock

1 Heat the oil in a large pan, add the onion and fry for about 10 minutes until soft.
Add the chillies and coriander seeds to the pan and cook for 1–2 minutes.

2 Add the squash, sweet potatoes and tomatoes and cook for 5 minutes. Add the
hot stock, then cover the pan and bring to the boil. Simmer gently for 15 minutes or
until the vegetables are soft.

3 Whiz the soup, in batches, in a blender or food processor until smooth. Adjust the
seasoning and reheat to serve.

Special roasted tomato and pepper soup

Serves 6

Hands-on time: 20 minutes

Cooking time: about 1 hour

240 cals, 17g fat (of which 6g saturates), 14g carbohydrate per serving

1.4kg (3lb) full-flavoured ripe tomatoes

2 red peppers, cored, deseeded and chopped

4 garlic cloves, peeled and crushed

3 small onions, thinly sliced

20g ($^3/_4$oz) thyme sprigs

4 tbsp olive oil

4 tbsp Worcestershire sauce

4 tbsp vodka

6 tbsp double cream

1 Preheat the oven to 200°C (180°C fan oven) mark 6. Remove any green stalk heads from the tomatoes and discard. Put the tomatoes into a large roasting tin with the peppers, garlic and onions. Scatter 6 thyme sprigs on top, drizzle with the olive oil and roast for 25 minutes. Turn the vegetables over and roast for a further 30–40 minutes until tender and slightly charred.

2 Put one-third of the vegetables into a blender or food processor with 300ml ($^1/_2$ pint) boiled water. Add the Worcestershire sauce, vodka, and seasoning if needed. Whiz until smooth, then press through a sieve into a pan.

3 Whiz the remaining vegetables with 450ml ($^3/_4$ pint) boiled water, then sieve and add to the pan.

4 To serve, warm the soup thoroughly, stirring occasionally. Pour into warmed bowls, add 1 tbsp double cream to each, then drag a cocktail stick through the cream to create a swirl. Scatter a few thyme leaves over the top to finish.

Cucumber, yogurt and mint soup

Serves 6

Hands-on time: 15 minutes

Cooking time: none

100 cals, 8g fat (of which 4g saturates), 2g carbohydrate per serving

1 cucumber, coarsely grated

500g (1lb 2oz) Greek-style yogurt

A generous handful of mint leaves, chopped

1 large garlic clove, peeled and crushed

125ml (4fl oz) cold water or light vegetable

  or chicken stock

to serve

6 ice cubes

6 mint sprigs

1 Put all the ingredients in a large bowl and mix together. Chill until required.

2 Before serving, stir the soup, then taste and adjust the seasoning. Spoon the soup into bowls and drop an ice cube and a mint sprig into each.

▼ COOK'S TIP

- Raw garlic is a wonderful tonic for your health and is world-renowned for its curative and protective powers, including lowering blood pressure and cholesterol levels.

- Fresh garlic has plump, juicy, mild cloves and is available from May throughout the summer. It is the classic form of garlic to use to make pesto, salsa verde, garlic mayonnaise and chilled soups. It is usually far more digestible than dried garlic, and is the best garlic to eat raw.

Creamy watercress soup

Serves 6

Hands-on time: 15 minutes

Cooking time: 30 minutes

270 cals, 13g fat (of which 8g saturates), 31g carbohydrate per serving

250g (9oz) watercress

50g (2oz) butter

1 onion, finely chopped

700g (1¹/₂lb) potatoes, cut into small pieces

900ml (1¹/₂ pints) milk

900ml (1¹/₂ pints) vegetable stock

6 tbsp single cream

1 Trim the watercress and discard coarse stalks. Reserve a few sprigs for the garnish and roughly chop the rest.

2 Melt the butter in a large pan, add the onion and cook gently for 8 10 minutes until soft. Add the potatoes and cook for 1 minute, then pour in the milk and stock and bring to the boil. Reduce the heat and cook for 15–20 minutes until tender.

3 Take the pan off the heat. Stir in the watercress, then transfer to a liquidizer and blend in batches until smooth. Pour the soup back into a clean pan.

4 Add the cream and season to taste. Heat through and serve with parmesan crisps (see page 57) if liked. Garnish with the reserved watercress sprigs.

Easy chicken salad

Serves 1

Hands-on time: 10 minutes

Cooking time: none

220 cals, 7g fat (of which 2g saturates), 17g carbohydrate per serving

100g (3$^{1}/_{2}$oz) shredded roast chicken, skin discarded

1 carrot, chopped

$^{1}/_{4}$ cucumber, chopped

Handful of ripe cherry tomatoes, chopped

1 tbsp hummus

Squeeze of lemon juice

1 Put the shredded roast chicken into a shallow bowl. Add the carrot, celery, cucumber and chopped cherry tomatoes.

2 Top with the hummus and a squeeze of lemon juice.

▼ VARIATION

- To make the salad even more nutritious, add a few pumpkin seeds or sunflower seeds.

- To pack a vitamin punch, include a handful of sprouted seeds such as alfalfa, or chopped watercress, with the chicken and salad vegetables.

- For extra bite, add a little finely chopped red chilli; for extra sweetness, add some strips of red pepper.

- For extra flavour, add some chopped coriander or torn basil leaves.

▼ COOK'S TIP

This salad makes an excellent packed lunch. Put in a sealed container.

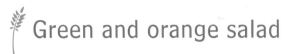

Green and orange salad

Serves 1

Hands-on time: 10 minutes

Cooking time: none

200 cals, 14g fat (of which 2g saturates), 13g carbohydrate per serving

1 organic orange

1 tsp olive oil

$^1/_2$ tsp white wine vinegar

$^1/_4$ avocado, sliced

1 little gem lettuce, leaves torn

Handful of chopped chives

Handful of watercress, washed and roughly chopped

2 tbsp low-fat cottage cheese or 75g (3oz) tuna in

   brine, drained, or 75g (3oz) roast chicken

1 Cut the rind and pith from the orange, then cut the flesh into segments. Put into a serving bowl and add the oil, white wine vinegar, sliced avocado, torn lettuce leaves, the chopped chives and watercress.

2 Toss together, arrange the cottage cheese, tuna or roast chicken on top and serve.

▼ **VARIATION**

For an easy dairy-free, low-GI or vegetarian salad, substitute half a can of drained, cooked mixed beans for the cottage cheese, tuna or chicken.

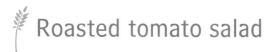

Roasted tomato salad

Serves 10

Hands-on time: 10 minutes, plus cooling time

Cooking time: 40–45 minutes

170 cals, 17g fat (of which 2g saturates), 4g carbohydrate per serving

900g (2lb) ripe plum tomatoes, halved

2 garlic cloves, peeled and sliced

5 tbsp extra-virgin olive oil

1 medium red chilli, deseeded and finely chopped

2 tbsp balsamic vinegar

3 ripe but firm avocados, peeled, stoned and
   thickly sliced

1 Preheat the oven to 200°C (180°C fan oven) mark 6. Put the tomatoes into a shallow roasting tin, cut-side up. Season with salt and pepper, scatter with garlic and drizzle with 2 tbsp olive oil. Roast in the oven for 40–45 minutes.

2 Meanwhile, make the salad dressing. In a large bowl, mix together the remaining oil, the chilli and balsamic vinegar.

3 Transfer the tomatoes and any cooking juices to a large serving platter and leave to cool. Add the avocado to the dressing and toss to coat. Spoon over the tomatoes and serve.

▼ COOK'S TIP

- Chillies vary enormously in strength from quite mild to blisteringly hot, depending on the type of chilli and its ripeness. Taste a small piece first, to check that it is not too hot for you.

- When handling chillies be extremely careful not to touch or rub your eyes with your fingers, as it will sting. Wash knives immediately after handling chillies for the same reason. As a precaution, use rubber gloves when preparing them, if you prefer.

Classic coleslaw

Serves 10

Hands-on time: 20 minutes

Cooking time: none

140 cals, 10g fat (of which 1g saturates), 8g carbohydrate per serving

$^1/_2$ each small red and white cabbage, shredded

2 carrots, grated

40g (1$^1/_2$oz) flat-leaved parsley, finely chopped

for the dressing

2$^1/_2$ tbsp red wine vinegar

125ml (4fl oz) olive oil

1 tbsp Dijon mustard

1 First, make the dressing. Pour the red wine vinegar into a large jam jar. Add the olive oil and mustard and season with salt and pepper. Screw on the lid and shake well.

2 Put the shredded cabbage and grated carrot into a large serving bowl. Toss everything together so the vegetables are well mixed.

3 Add the parsley. Shake the dressing again, pour it over the cabbage mixture, then toss well to coat. Serve.

▼ **COOK'S TIP**

Use a food processor to prepare the vegetables. The slicing attachment (for the cabbage) and grater (for the carrots) will make light work of this quantity of vegetables.

Griddled polenta with gorgonzola salad

Serves 4

Hands-on time: 20 minutes, plus cooling time

Cooking time: 20 minutes

410 cals, 26g fat (of which 13g saturates), 31g carbohydrate food

Oil, to oil

300ml ($^1/_2$ pint) semi-skimmed milk

10 sage leaves, roughly chopped

125g (4oz) quick-cook polenta

2 garlic cloves, peeled and crushed

2 tbsp olive oil

25g (1oz) butter

100g (3$^1/_2$oz) salad leaves

125g (4oz) Gorgonzola cheese, cut into cubes

125g (4oz) each sunblush tomatoes and peppers

1 Lightly oil a 450g (1lb) loaf tin. Put the milk in a pan, then add the sage, 1 scant tsp salt and 300ml ($^1/_2$ pint) water and bring to the boil. Add the polenta to the pan in a thin, steady stream, stirring, to make a smooth paste.

2 Reduce the heat, add the garlic and cook for about 8 minutes, stirring occasionally. Add the oil, then season with pepper and stir well. Press into the prepared loaf tin, smooth the top and leave to cool for 45 minutes.

3 Once the polenta is cool, turn out on to a board and cut into eight slices.

4 Melt the butter in a griddle pan and fry the polenta slices on each side until golden.

5 Divide among four plates. Add the salad, Gorgonzola, sunblush tomatoes and peppers, and serve.

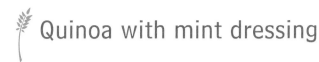

Quinoa with mint dressing

Serves 4
Hands-on time: 15 minutes
Cooking time: none
340 cals, 17g fat (of which 2g saturates), 40g carbohydrate per serving

250g (9oz) quinoa

400ml (14fl oz) hot vegetable or chicken stock

4 spring onions, finely chopped

20g (³/₄oz) mint, finely chopped

25g (1oz) pine nuts, toasted

2 tbsp lemon juice

3 tbsp olive oil

1 Cook the quinoa in a pan, uncovered, with the stock. When tender, about 10–12 minutes, drain thoroughly and turn into a bowl.

2 Finely chop the spring onions and mint. Add to the bowl with the toasted pine nuts, lemon juice and olive oil. Stir until well mixed and season lightly. Serve with kebabs, grilled poultry, fish or salad.

Warm lentil, chicken and broccoli salad

Serves 4

Hands-on time: 20 minutes

Cooking time: 30 minutes

350 cals, 18g fat (of which 3g saturates), 19g carbohydrate per serving

125g (4oz) Puy lentils

225g (8oz) broccoli

1 large garlic clove (see page 68)

1 tsp English mustard powder

2 tbsp balsamic vinegar

4 tbsp olive oil

1 red onion

350g (12oz) smoked chicken breast

1 Cook the lentils according to the packet instructions. Chop the broccoli and blanch in a pan of boiling water for 2 minutes. Drain, rinse and set aside.

2 Peel and crush the garlic then put into a bowl. Use a wooden spoon to combine it with a pinch of salt until creamy, then whisk in the mustard, vinegar and 3 tbsp olive oil. Set aside.

3 Peel and slice the onion. Heat the remaining oil in a frying pan, add the onion and cook for 5 minutes until softened.

4 Add the chicken and broccoli and stir-fry for 1–2 minutes. Stir in the lentils and dressing.

Pasta salad with sun-dried tomatoes

Serves 4

Hands-on time: 15 minutes, plus standing time

Cooking time: 10 minutes

360 cals, 21g fat (of which 3g saturates), 38g carbohydrate per serving

175g (6oz) dried gluten-free pasta shapes, such

   as penne

1 tbsp extra-virgin olive oil

4 sun-dried tomatoes in oil, drained and sliced

225g (8oz) cherry tomatoes, halved

4–6 spring onions, shredded

8–12 black olives

8–12 basil leaves, torn

for the dressing

2 sun-dried tomatoes in oil, drained

2 tbsp oil from sun-dried tomato jar

2 tbsp red wine vinegar

1 garlic clove, peeled (see page 68)

1 tbsp sun-dried tomato paste

Pinch of sugar (optional)

2 tbsp extra-virgin olive oil

1 Cook the pasta in a large pan of salted boiling water until *al dente*. Drain in a colander, refresh under cold running water, then drain thoroughly. Tip the pasta into a large bowl and toss with the olive oil to prevent sticking.

2 Add the sun-dried tomatoes, cherry tomatoes, spring onions, olives and torn basil leaves. Toss to mix with the pasta.

3 To make the dressing, put the sun-dried tomatoes and oil, wine vinegar, garlic and tomato paste into a blender or food processor. Add the sugar, if using. With the motor running, pour the olive oil through the feeder tube and process briefly to make a fairly thick dressing. Season to taste.

4 Pour the dressing over the pasta and toss well. Cover and leave to stand for 1–2 hours before serving if possible, to allow the flavours to develop.

Japanese noodle salad

Serves 8
Hands-on time time: 2 minutes
Cooking time: 5 minutes
140 cals, 5g fat (of which 1g saturates), 20g carbohydrate per serving

2 level tbsp sesame seeds

200g (7oz) Japanese wheat-free soba noodles

2–3 tbsp tamari (wheat-free Japanese soy sauce)

1 tbsp sesame oil

1 tbsp rice vinegar

1 Dry-fry the sesame seeds in a frying pan until golden. Set aside.

2 Cook the noodles in a pan of salted boiling water for 5 minutes or until tender but firm. Drain and cool under cold running water. Drain again and put into a bowl.

3 Add the toasted sesame seeds, tamari, oil and the rice vinegar and toss to coat the noodles. Chill until needed or for up to 24 hours.

▼ **VARIATION**

Thinly sliced mushrooms, diced red pepper, cubes of tofu or cooked broccoli or asparagus spears can all be added. Add to the salad just before serving, and mix well.

Mild spiced chicken and quinoa

Serves 4

Hands-on time: 15 minutes

Cooking time: 30 minutes

300 cals, 8g fat (of which 2g saturates), 34g carbohydrate per serving

2 tbsp mango chutney

Juice of $^1/_2$ organic lemon

1 tbsp olive oil

2 tsp mild curry powder

1 tsp paprika

350g (12oz) skinless, boneless chicken breast,
    cut into thick strips

200g (7oz) quinoa

1 cucumber, roughly chopped

$^1/_2$ bunch spring onions, sliced

60g (2oz) ready-to-eat dried apricots, sliced

2 tbsp chopped mint, basil or tarragon

1 Put the chutney, lemon juice, $^1/_2$ tbsp oil, curry powder and paprika into a bowl and mix together. Add the chicken and toss to coat.

2 Cook the quinoa in boiling water for 10–12 minutes until tender (or following packet instructions). Drain thoroughly. Put into a bowl, then stir in the cucumber, spring onions, apricots, herbs and remaining oil.

3 Put the chicken and marinade into a pan and fry over a high heat for 2–3 minutes, then add 150ml ($^1/_4$ pint) water. Bring to the boil, then simmer for 5 minutes or until the chicken is cooked. Serve with the quinoa.

Easy suppers

The recipes in this chapter are all designed to be made as easily as possible, whether you're coming in at the end of a long day and need a satisfying meal without too much stress or are cooking for the family.

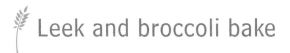

Leek and broccoli bake

Serves 4

Hands-on time: 20 minutes

Cooking time: 45–55 minutes

220 cals, 12g fat (of which 4g saturates), 15g carbohydrate per serving

2 tbsp olive oil

1 large red onion, peeled and cut into wedges

1 aubergine, chopped

2 leeks, cut into chunks

1 broccoli head, cut into florets and stalks chopped

3 large flat mushrooms, chopped

2 x 400g cans cherry tomatoes

3 rosemary sprigs, chopped

50g (2oz) Parmesan cheese, freshly grated

1 Preheat the oven to 200°C (180°C fan oven) mark 6. Heat the oil in a large flameproof dish, add the onion, aubergine and leeks and cook for 10–12 minutes until golden and softened.

2 Add the remaining vegetables, the cherry tomatoes, half the rosemary and 300ml (½ pint) boiling water. Season with salt and pepper. Stir well, then cover and cook in the oven for 30 minutes.

3 Meanwhile, put the Parmesan into a bowl. Add the remaining rosemary and season with pepper. When the vegetables are cooked, remove the lid and sprinkle the Parmesan mixture on top. Cook, uncovered, in the oven for a further 5–10 minutes until the topping is golden.

Chickpea curry

Serves 6

Hands-on time: 20 minutes

Cooking time: about 25 minutes

230 cals, 8g fat (of which 1g saturates), 31g carbohydrate per serving

2 tbsp vegetable oil

2 onions, peeled and finely chopped

2 garlic cloves, peeled and sliced

1 tbsp ground coriander

1 tsp mild chilli powder

1 tsp black mustard seeds

2 tbsp sun-dried tomato paste

300g (11oz) new potatoes, quartered

400g (14oz) canned chopped tomatoes

1 litre (1³/₄ pints) hot vegetable stock

250g (9oz) green beans, trimmed

2 × 400g (14oz) cans chickpeas, drained

2 tsp garam masala

1 Heat the oil in a pan, add the onions and fry until golden. Add the garlic, coriander, chilli powder, mustard seeds and tomato paste and cook for 1–2 minutes, stirring.

2 Add the potatoes, tomatoes and stock, and check the seasoning. Cover and bring to the boil, then simmer, half-covered, for 20 minutes.

3 Add the green beans and chickpeas and cook for 5 minutes. Stir in the garam masala and serve with rice and natural yogurt.

Baked eggs

Serves 2

Hands-on time: 15 minutes

Cooking time: 15 minutes

270 cals, 24g fat (of which 6g saturates), 3g carbohydrate per serving

2 tbsp olive oil

125g (4oz) mushrooms, chopped

225g (8oz) fresh spinach

2 eggs

2 tbsp single cream

1 Preheat the oven to 200°C (180°C fan oven) mark 6. Heat the oil in a large frying pan, add the chopped mushrooms and stir-fry for 30 seconds. Add the spinach and stir-fry until wilted. Season to taste, then divide the mixture between two shallow ovenproof dishes.

2 Carefully break the eggs into the centre of each dish, then spoon 1 tbsp single cream over each.

3 Cook in the oven for about 12 minutes until just set – the eggs will continue to cook a little once they're out of the oven. Grind a little more pepper, if liked, over the top and serve.

Asparagus risotto

Serves 4

Hands-on time: 10 minutes

Cooking time: 25 minutes

450 cals, 21g fat (of which 13g saturates), 49g carbohydrate per serving

50g (2oz) butter

2 shallots, peeled and diced

2 garlic cloves, peeled and crushed

225g (8oz) arborio (risotto) rice

500ml (16fl oz) vegetable or chicken stock

2 tbsp Mascarpone cheese

50g (2oz) Parmesan cheese, finely grated, plus

   shavings to garnish

2 tbsp chopped parsley

400g (14oz) asparagus spears, blanched and halved

1 Melt the butter in a pan with a heavy base, add the shallots and garlic, and sauté over a gentle heat until soft.

2 Stir in the rice, cook for 1–2 minutes, then add the stock. Bring to the boil and simmer for 15–20 minutes, stirring occasionally to ensure that the rice isn't sticking, until almost all the stock has been absorbed and the rice is tender.

3 Add the Mascarpone, half the Parmesan and half the parsley to the pan. Stir in the asparagus, remaining parsley and the Parmesan. Spoon on to plates, garnish with shavings of Parmesan and serve.

Stuffed peppers

Serves 4
Hands-on time: 20 minutes
Cooking time: 55 minutes
310 cals, 6g fat (of which 1g saturates), 62g carbohydrate per serving

225g (8oz) brown basmati rice

1 tbsp olive oil

2 medium onions, peeled and chopped

400g can cherry tomatoes

3 tbsp chopped coriander

4 red peppers, halved and deseeded, leaving

  stalks intact

150ml ($^1/_4$ pint) hot vegetable stock

1 Preheat the oven to 200°C (180°C fan oven) mark 6. Cook the rice according to the packet instructions. Drain.

2 Meanwhile, heat the oil in a pan, add the onions and fry for 15 minutes. Add the tomatoes and leave to simmer for 10 minutes. Stir in the cooked rice and coriander, then spoon the mixture into the halved peppers.

3 Put the peppers into a roasting tin and pour the stock around the peppers. Roast in the oven for 30 minutes until tender.

▼ **VARIATION**

  Add 25g (1oz) pine nuts or chopped cashew nuts to the cooked rice and coriander at step 2.

Smoked sesame tofu

Serves 4

Hands-on time: 20 minutes, plus marinating time

Cooking time: 12 minutes

210 cals, 11g fat (of which 1g saturates), 18g carbohydrate per serving

2 tbsp toasted sesame seeds

2 tbsp tamari (wheat-free Japanese soy sauce)

1 tsp light muscovado sugar

1 tsp rice wine vinegar

1 tbsp sesame oil

225g (8oz) smoked tofu, cubed

$^{1}/_{2}$ small white or green cabbage, shredded

2 carrots, cut into strips

200g (7oz) beansprouts

4 roasted red peppers, roughly chopped
   (available in jars)

2 spring onions, shredded

1 Put the sesame seeds into a bowl, add the tamari sauce, sugar, vinegar and $^{1}/_{2}$ tbsp sesame oil. Mix together, then add the smoked tofu and stir to coat. Set aside to marinate for 10 minutes.

2 Heat a large wok or non-stick frying pan, add the marinated tofu, reserving the marinade, and fry for 5 minutes until golden all over. Remove from the wok with a slotted spoon and set aside.

3 Heat the remaining oil in the wok, add the cabbage and carrots and stir-fry for 5 minutes. Stir in the beansprouts, peppers, spring onions, cooked tofu and reserved marinade and cook for a further 2 minutes. Serve immediately with brown rice.

Chilli bolognese

Serves 4

Hands-on time: 15 minutes

Cooking time: 26–38 minutes

400 cals, 23g fat (of which 9g saturates), 12g carbohydrate per serving

1 tbsp olive oil

1 large onion, peeled and finely chopped

$^1/_2$ large red chilli (see page 74), deseeded and
thinly sliced

450g (1lb) lean best-quality minced beef or lamb

125g (4oz) smoked bacon lardons

3 roasted red peppers, drained and finely chopped

400g (14oz) canned chopped tomatoes

125ml (4fl oz) red wine

300g (11oz) dried wheat-free spaghetti

25g (1oz) freshly grated Cheddar or Gruyère cheese

2 tbsp chopped flat-leaved parsley (optional)

1 Heat the oil in a large pan over a medium heat, add the onion and chilli and fry for 5–10 minutes until soft and golden. Add the minced beef and lardons and stir over the heat for 5–7 minutes until well browned.

2 Stir in the red pepper, tomatoes and red wine. Season with pepper, if liked, bring to the boil, then simmer over a low heat for 15–20 minutes.

3 Meanwhile, cook the pasta according to the packet instructions. Drain.

4 Just before serving, stir the sauce into the spagetti, then add the grated cheese and parsley, if using.

Courgette and anchovy pasta sauce

Serves 4

Hands-on time: 10 minutes

Cooking time: 15 minutes

60 cals, 3g fat (of which trace saturates), 4g carbohydrate per serving

50g (2oz) canned anchovies in oil

1 garlic clove, peeled and crushed

Pinch of dried chilli

400ml (14fl oz) passata

2 courgettes, diced

1 Gently heat the oil from the can of anchovies in a frying pan. Add the garlic and dried chilli and cook for 1 minute.

2 Add the passata, courgettes and anchovies. Bring to the boil and simmer for about 10 minutes until the anchovies have melted, stirring well.

▼ **COOK'S TIP**

Toss with 300g (11oz) of cooked wheat-free penne.

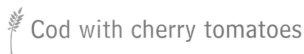

Cod with cherry tomatoes

Serves 4

Hands-on time: 15 minutes

Cooking time: about 25 minutes

180 cals, 8g fat (of which 1g saturates), 8g carbohydrate per serving

4 × 100g (3½oz) cod steaks

1 tbsp gluten-free flour

2 tbsp olive oil

1 small onion, sliced

1 large red chilli (see page 74), deseeded
  and chopped

1 garlic clove, crushed

250g (9oz) cherry tomatoes, halved

4 spring onions, chopped

2 tbsp chopped coriander

1 Season the cod with salt and pepper, then lightly dust with the flour. Heat 1 tbsp oil in a large frying pan, add the onion and fry for 5–10 minutes until golden.

2 Pour the remaining oil into the pan. Add the cod and fry for 3 minutes on each side. Add the chilli, garlic, cherry tomatoes, spring onions and coriander, and season with salt and pepper. Cover and continue to cook for 5–10 minutes until everything is heated through.

Peppered tuna with olive and herb salsa

Serves 4

Hands-on time: 15 minutes

Cooking time: 8–12 minutes

250 cals, 11g fat (of which 3g saturates), 0g carbohydrate per serving

1 tsp olive oil

Zest and juice of 1 organic lime

1 tbsp cracked mixed peppercorns

4 × 150g (5oz) tuna steaks

for the olive and herb salsa

1 tbsp extra-virgin olive oil

1 tbsp each black and green olives, roughly chopped

Zest and juice of $^{1}/_{2}$ organic lemon

2 tbsp chopped parsley

1 tbsp chopped coriander

1 tbsp capers, roughly chopped

1 Put the olive oil into a large, shallow bowl, then add the lime zest and juice and peppercorns. Add the tuna and toss to coat.

2 Heat a non-stick griddle pan until hot. Cook the tuna steaks, two at a time, for 2–3 minutes on each side.

3 Put all the ingredients for the salsa in a bowl and mix together. Season to taste and mix well, then serve with the tuna.

Salmon kedgeree

Serves 4

Hands-on time: 15 minutes, plus soaking time

Cooking time: 50 minutes

540 cals, 21g fat (of which 9g saturates), 67g carbohydrate per serving

50g (2oz) butter

700g (1½lb) onions, sliced

2 level tsp garam masala

1 garlic clove, crushed

75g (3oz) split green lentils, soaked in 300ml (½ pint)
   boiling water for 15 minutes, then drained

750ml (1¼ pints) vegetable stock

225g (8oz) basmati rice

1 medium green chilli (see page 74), deseeded
   and finely chopped

350g (12oz) salmon fillet

Coriander sprigs, to garnish

1 Melt the butter in a flameproof casserole, add the onions and cook gently for about 5 minutes, until soft. Remove one-third and set aside. Increase the heat and cook the remaining onions for 10 minutes to caramelize. Remove and set aside.

2 Return the first batch of onions to the casserole, add the garam masala and garlic and cook, stirring, for 1 minute. Add the drained lentils and stock, cover and cook for 15 minutes. Add the rice and chilli, season with salt and pepper, bring to the boil, cover and simmer for 5 minutes.

3 Put the salmon fillet on top of the rice, cover and continue to cook gently for 15 minutes, until the rice is cooked, the stock absorbed and the salmon opaque.

4 Lift off the salmon and divide into flakes. Return the salmon to the casserole and fork through the rice. Garnish with reserved caramelized onions and coriander, and serve.

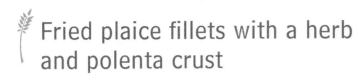

Fried plaice fillets with a herb and polenta crust

Serves 2

Hands-on time: 10–14 minutes

Cooking time: 6 minutes

410 cals, 20g fat (of which 3g saturates), 19g carbohydrate per serving

1 tsp finely chopped rosemary or 1 tsp finely

  snipped chives

1 tsp finely chopped thyme

2 garlic cloves, peeled and very finely chopped

50g (2oz) polenta

Finely grated zest and juice of 2 small organic lemons

2 plaice fillets, about 175g (6oz) each, skinned

1 large egg

2 tbsp olive oil

1 Combine the herbs, garlic and polenta on a flat plate. Add the lemon zest, salt and pepper and mix well. Wipe the plaice fillets with kitchen paper.

2 Beat the egg in a shallow dish, dip the fish fillets in the egg and coat them with the polenta mixture, pressing it on well.

3 Heat the oil in a very large frying pan over a high heat. When hot, add the fish, turn the heat down to medium and cook for about 2–3 minutes on each side, depending on the thickness of the fillets. Drain on kitchen paper and serve on hot plates with the lemon juice poured over them.

Turkey and sesame stir-fry with noodles

Serves 4
Hands-on time: 5 minutes
Cooking time: 10 minutes
660 cals, 15g fat (of which 2g saturates), 100g carbohydrate per serving

300g (11oz) turkey breast meat

3 tbsp tamari (wheat-free Japanese soy sauce)

3 level tbsp runny honey

300g (11oz) rice or cellophane noodles

1 tbsp sesame oil, plus extra for the noodles

2 tbsp sesame seeds

300g (11oz) mixed stir-fry vegetables (e.g. red
   peppers, carrots, celery, mangetout, beansprouts)

   sliced into thin strips

1 Put the turkey strips into a large bowl with the tamari marinade and honey, and stir to coat. Cover and set aside for 5 minutes to allow the flavours to soak in.

2 Toast the sesame seeds in a dry wok over a medium heat, stirring until they turn golden. Tip on to a plate.

3 Bring a pan of water to the boil and cook the noodles according to the packet instructions. Drain well, then toss in a little sesame oil.

4 While the noodles are cooking, heat 1 tbsp of the oil in the same wok and add the turkey, reserving the marinade. Stir-fry over a very high heat for 2–3 minutes until cooked through and beginning to brown.

5 Add a little more oil, if needed, then add the vegetables and leftover marinade. Continue to cook over a high heat, stirring, until the vegetables have started to soften and the sauce is warmed through.

6 Scatter with the sesame seeds and serve immediately with the noodles.

Calf's liver with fried sage and balsamic vinegar

Serves 4

Hands-on time: 20 minutes, plus standing time

Cooking time: 25 minutes

340 cals, 24g fat (of which 13g saturates), 8g carbohydrate per serving

12 sage leaves

4 slices of calf's liver

15g (¹/₂ oz) butter plus a little olive oil for frying

1–2 tbsp balsamic vinegar

1 Melt the butter with a little oil in a frying pan with a heavy base, and when hot add the sage leaves. Cook briefly for 1 minute or so until crisp. Remove, put in a single layer in a shallow dish and keep hot in the oven.

2 Add a little extra oil to the pan, put in 2 slices of calf's liver and cook quickly for 30 seconds on each side over a high heat. Remove and place on a plate while you quickly cook the remaining 2 slices.

3 Return all 4 slices to the pan, splash the balsamic vinegar over the top and cook for another minute or so.

4 Serve immediately with rice, wheat-free pasta or grilled polenta.

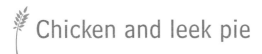

Chicken and leek pie

Serves 4

Hands-on time: 10 minutes

Cooking time: 40–45 minutes

470 cals, 14g fat (of which 7g saturates), 54g carbohydrate per serving

5 large potatoes

200g (7oz) crème fraîche

3 chicken breasts with skin

3 large leeks

About 10 tarragon leaves

1 Preheat the oven to 200°C (180°C fan oven) mark 6. Peel and chop the potatoes into chunks, then put into a pan of salted cold water. Cover, bring to the boil and simmer for 10–12 minutes until soft. Drain and return to the pan. Add 1 tbsp crème fraîche, season with salt and pepper, and mash well.

2 Meanwhile, heat a frying pan, then add the chicken, skin-side down, and fry gently for 5 minutes until the skin is golden. Turn and fry for 6–8 minutes on the other side. While the chicken is cooking, chop the leeks into chunks and finely chop the tarragon.

3 Remove the chicken from the pan and put on a board. Tip the chopped leeks into the pan and cook in the chicken juices over a low heat for 5 minutes to soften.

4 Discard the chicken skin and cut the flesh into bite-sized pieces (don't worry if it is not quite cooked through). Return the chicken to the pan, stir in the remaining crème fraîche and heat for 2–3 minutes until bubbling. Stir in the tarragon, season to taste, then spoon into a 1.7-litre (3-pint) ovenproof dish. Spread the mash on top.

5 Cook in the oven for 20–25 minutes until golden and heated through.

Sweet chilli beef stir-fry

Serves 4

Hands-on time: 10 minutes

Cooking time: 10–11 minutes

200 cals, 7g fat (of which 2g saturates), 8g carbohydrate per serving

1 tsp chilli oil

1 tbsp each tamari (wheat-free Japanese soy sauce)
  and runny honey

1 garlic clove, peeled and crushed

1 large red chilli (see page 74), halved, deseeded
  and chopped

400g (14oz) lean beef, cut into strips

1 tsp sunflower oil

1 broccoli head, shredded

200g (7oz) mangetout, halved

1 red pepper, halved, deseeded and cut into strips

1 Pour the chilli oil into a medium-sized shallow bowl. Add the tamari sauce, honey, garlic and chilli and stir well. Add the strips of beef and toss in the marinade.

2 Heat the sunflower oil in a wok over a high heat until it is very hot. Cook the strips of beef in two batches, for 3–4 minutes, or until just cooked through, then remove them from the wok and set aside. Wipe the wok with kitchen paper to remove any residue.

3 Add the broccoli, mangetout, red pepper and 2 tbsp water and stir-fry for 5–6 minutes until starting to soften. Return the beef to the wok to heat through. Serve with rice.

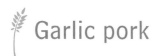

Garlic pork

Serves 4
Hands-on time: 8 minutes
Cooking time: 16–22 minutes
260 cals, 14g fat (of which 5g saturates), 0g carbohydrate per serving

1 tbsp olive oil

2 garlic cloves, peeled and crushed

5cm (2in) piece fresh root ginger, peeled and grated

4 pork chops

1 Preheat the grill to high. Put the oil into a small bowl, add the garlic and ginger and a pinch of salt, and stir well to mix.

2 Grill the pork chops for 7–10 minutes on each side, then remove from the grill. Brush the oil mixture all over the chops, then return to the grill and cook for a further 2 minutes on each side. Serve with stir-fried shredded cabbage.

Moroccan spiced chicken kebabs

Serves 4

Hands-on time: 10 minutes, plus marinating time

Cooking time: 10–12 minutes

240 cals, 13g fat (of which 3g saturates), 0g carbohydrate per serving

2 tbsp olive oil

15g (1/2oz) flat-leaved parsley

1 garlic clove, peeled

1/2 tsp paprika

1 tsp ground cumin

Zest and juice of 1 organic lemon

4 skinless chicken breasts, cut into bite-sized chunks

1 Put the oil into a blender and add the parsley, garlic, paprika, cumin, lemon zest and juice, and a pinch of salt. Whiz to make a paste.

2 Put the chicken into a medium-sized shallow dish and rub in the spice paste. Leave to marinate for at least 20 minutes. Preheat the grill to high.

3 Thread the marinated chicken on to skewers and grill for 10–12 minutes, turning every now and then, until the meat is cooked through. Serve with shredded lettuce, sliced tomatoes and sliced cucumber.

Food for friends

Cooking and sharing a meal with friends is one of life's great pleasures. Wheat-free entertaining, whether it's a simple supper or more formal meal, is easy. Food for friends shows you how.

Scallops with sweet-and-sour cucumber and pickled ginger

Smoked mackerel pâté

Trout and dill fishcakes

Baked anchovy potatoes and parsnips

Salmon with a spicy yogurt crust

Oriental beef salad

Roasted cod with fennel

Vegetable moussaka

Squash and pancetta risotto

Warming winter casserole

Venison sausages with red onion marmalade

Pot-roasted pheasant with red cabbage

Lean lamb and tomato gratin

One-pot chicken

Beef with beer and mushrooms

Curried lamb with lentils

Braised lamb shanks with cannellini beans

Scallops with sweet-and-sour cucumber and pickled ginger

Serves 6

Hands-on time: 20 minutes, plus chilling time

Cooking time: none

280 cals, 7g fat (of which 1g saturates), 6g carbohydrate per serving

18 large fresh scallops, without roe, well chilled

Juice of 2 limes

2 level tbsp golden caster sugar

1 tbsp white wine vinegar

$^1/_2$ cucumber, deseeded and diced

2 tbsp mild extra-virgin olive oil

Pickled ginger

A bunch of watercress, well washed, to garnish

1 Trim and discard any hard muscle from the side of the scallops, then slice each one very thinly crossways. Arrange in a single layer on a large plate and squeeze the juice of $1^1/_2$ limes over the top. Cover and chill for 2 hours.

2 Put the sugar, a pinch of salt, plenty of pepper and 2 tbsp boiling water into a bowl, then stir to dissolve the sugar. Mix in the vinegar, add the cucumber, cover the bowl and chill for 1 hour.

3 Pour the remaining lime juice into a small bowl, add a pinch of salt and a little pepper and whisk. Whisk in the oil to make a dressing.

4 Remove the scallops from the lime juice and arrange the slices in pairs on individual plates. Using a slotted spoon, put some drained cucumber in the centre and top with slivers of pickled ginger. Drizzle the dressing over the scallops and arrange watercress sprigs around them.

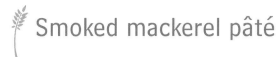

Smoked mackerel pâté

Serves 4

Hands-on time: 15 minutes

Cooking time: none

280 cals, 22g fat (of which 5g saturates), 3g carbohydrate per serving

3 smoked mackerel fillets, skinned

150g (5oz) Greek-style yogurt

2 tbsp horseradish sauce

Juice of $\frac{1}{2}$ organic lemon

Pinch of cayenne pepper

Lemon wedges, to serve

1 Roughly break the fish into a food processor. Add the Greek yogurt and horseradish sauce and whiz together. Add lemon juice, pepper and pinch of cayenne pepper. Stir to mix, then spoon the pâté into individual ramekins and sprinkle with a little more cayenne. Serve with wheat-free toast, rocket and lemon wedges.

Trout and dill fishcakes

Serves 4

Hands-on time: 15 minutes

Cooking time: 25 minutes

280 cals, 7g fat (of which 1g saturates), 38g carbohydrate per serving

4 medium-sized potatoes

2 trout fillets

3 spring onions

2 dill sprigs

1 organic lemon

1 tbsp olive oil

A little plain gluten-free flour

1 Peel and chop the potatoes and cook in a pan of salted boiling water for 6–8 minutes until tender. Drain, return to the pan and mash.

2 Preheat the grill to high. Grill the trout fillets for 8–10 minutes until cooked through and firm to the touch. Skin the fish, flake into pieces, removing any bones, then put into the pan with the mashed potato.

3 Cut the spring onions into small pieces, chop the dill sprigs and zest the lemon. Add to the pan with the olive oil and mix together well.

4 Shape the mixture into eight small patties. Dust with flour and put on a non-stick baking sheet, then grill for a further 3 minutes on each side. Serve the fishcakes with a watercress salad.

▼ **VARIATION**

Replace trout with 225g (8oz) of cooked salmon, haddock or smoked haddock. Skin, flake and add at stage 2 as before.

Baked anchovy potatoes and parsnips

Serves 6 as a side dish

Hands-on time: 20 minutes

Cooking time: 1 hour 20 minutes

90 cals, 14g fat (of which 2g saturates), 36g carbohydrate per serving

3 tbsp olive oil

450g (1lb) each potatoes and parsnips

450ml (3/4 pint) hot vegetable or chicken stock

1 tbsp Dijon mustard

1 small onion, peeled and finely sliced

1 garlic clove, peeled

50g (2oz) canned anchovies in oil

Small handful of flat-leaved parsley

1 Preheat the oven to 190°C (170°C fan oven) mark 5. Grease a 2-litre (3½-pint) ovenproof dish with 1 tbsp olive oil. Peel and cut the potatoes and parsnips into bite-sized chunks.

2 Pour the stock into a pan, add the Dijon mustard and bring to the boil. Add the potatoes and parsnips, return to the boil then remove from the heat. Season with pepper.

3 Heat 2 tbsp olive oil in a frying pan, add the onion and cook gently for 10 minutes until softened. Crush the garlic, add to the onion and cook for 1–2 minutes. Remove from the heat. Drain and chop the anchovies and add to the onion.

4 Put half the potatoes, parsnips and stock into the ovenproof dish, spoon over the onion and anchovy mixture over it, then cover with the remaining potatoes, parsnips and stock.

5 Cook, uncovered, in the oven for 1 hour or until tender and golden. Chop the parsley and sprinkle it over just before serving. Serve with roast chicken and freshly cooked spinach.

Salmon with a spicy yogurt crust

Serves 4

Hands-on time: 10 minutes

Cooking time: about 10 minutes

250 cals, 15g fat (of which 4g saturates), 3g carbohydrate per serving

3 tbsp chopped coriander

1 garlic clove, peeled and crushed

2.5cm (1in) piece fresh root ginger, peeled
  and grated

$^1/_2$ tsp each ground cumin and coriander

$^1/_4$ tsp cayenne pepper

150g (5oz) natural yogurt

4 × 125g (4oz) salmon fillets

1 Preheat the grill. Mix together the chopped coriander, garlic, ginger, cumin, ground coriander, cayenne, pinch of salt and yogurt. Add the salmon and turn to coat.

2 Grill the fish for 7–10 minutes or until cooked through. Serve with 50g (2oz) rice per person, cooked according to the packet instructions. Also serve a herb salad and lime wedges to squeeze over the fish.

Oriental beef salad

Serves 4

Hands-on time: 10 minutes

Cooking time: about 10 minutes

210 cals, 10g fat (of which 3g saturates), 10g carbohydrate per serving

4 tbsp tamari (wheat-free Japanese soy sauce)

Juice of $1/2$ lime

2 × 175g (6oz) sirloin steaks

1 tbsp vegetable oil

1 mango, peeled, stoned and sliced

4 spring onions, sliced

$1/2$ Chinese lettuce, finely sliced

150g (5oz) beansprouts

1 tbsp sesame seeds, toasted

2 tbsp chopped coriander

1 In a bowl, mix together the tamari sauce and lime juice. Spoon half the dressing over the steaks and set the remainder aside.

2 Heat the oil in a frying pan, add the steaks and fry for 2 minutes on each side for medium rare, or 3–4 minutes for well done. Set aside.

3 Put the mango, spring onions, lettuce and beansprouts into a large bowl. Slice the steak into 1cm ($1/2$in) strips, add to the bowl with the remaining dressing and sprinkle with sesame seeds and coriander to serve.

Roasted cod with fennel

Serves 4

Hands-on time: 3 minutes

Cooking time: 17 minutes

270 cals, 15g fat (of which 7g saturates), 7g carbohydrate per serving

50g (2oz) butter

1 tbsp olive oil

2 medium red onions, finely sliced

2 small or 1 large fennel bulb, trimmed and

    finely sliced

2 tbsp chopped dill, plus extra to sprinkle

150ml (5fl oz) of a fruity white wine

4 × 150g (5oz) pieces of Icelandic cod

1 Preheat the oven to 200°C (180°C fan oven) mark 6. Heat the butter and oil in a flameproof casserole dish over a medium heat. When sizzling, add the onions and fennel, then cover and cook, stirring occasionally, for 7 minutes or until soft and translucent.

2 Add the dill and wine and bring quickly to the boil. Sit the fish on top of the fennel mixture and season with salt and pepper. Put the casserole dish in the oven and cook for 10 minutes, basting the fish occasionally with the juices.

3 Sprinkle with plenty of extra dill and serve immediately with new potatoes and green beans.

Vegetable moussaka

Serves 6

Hands-on time: 45 minutes

Cooking time: 1 hour 30 minutes

340 cals, 21g fat (of which 8g saturates), 23g carbohydrate per serving

450g (1lb) potatoes, cut lengthways into
  5mm (¼ in) slices

1 aubergine, sliced into rounds

1 large red onion, cut into wedges

2 red peppers, deseeded and sliced

4 tbsp olive oil

2 level tbsp chopped thyme

225g (8oz) tomatoes, thickly sliced

2 garlic cloves, peeled and sliced

250g (9oz) passata

250g (9oz) carton soft goat's cheese

300ml (½ pint) natural yogurt

3 medium eggs

25g (1oz) freshly grated Parmesan cheese

1 Preheat the oven to 230°C (210°C fan oven) mark 8. Boil the potatoes in a pan of salted water for 5 minutes. Drain and put into a large roasting tin with the aubergine, onion and peppers. Drizzle with oil, add the thyme, toss and season with salt and pepper. Roast for 30 minutes, stirring occasionally.

2 Add the tomato and garlic and roast for 15 minutes, then take out of the oven. Reduce the oven temperature to 200°C (180°C fan oven) mark 6.

3 Put half the vegetables in a 1.7-litre (3-pint) ovenproof dish, then spoon half the passata over them and spread the goat's cheese on top. Repeat with the rest of the vegetables and passata. Mix together the yogurt, eggs and Parmesan. Season and then pour over the top. Cook in the oven for 45 minutes or until heated through.

Squash and pancetta risotto

Serves 4

Hands-on time: 10 minutes

Cooking time: about 40 minutes

460 cals; 13g fat (of which 5g saturates), 74g carbohydrate

125g (4oz) pancetta or smoked bacon

1 small butternut squash

1 onion, chopped

300g (11oz) arborio (risotto) rice

1 litre (1¾ pints) hot vegetable stock

1 Chop the pancetta. Peel and cut the squash into small chunks, then put both into a large, deep frying pan and fry over a medium heat for 8–10 minutes.

2 Meanwhile, finely chop the onion and, when the pancetta is golden and the squash has softened, add to the pan and continue to fry for 5 minutes until softened.

3 Stir in the rice, cook for 1–2 minutes, then add the stock. Bring to the boil and simmer for 15–20 minutes, stirring occasionally to ensure that the rice doesn't stick, until almost all the stock has been absorbed and the rice and squash are tender.

Warming winter casserole

Serves 4
Hands-on time: 20 minutes
Cooking time: 1 hour
400 cals; 21g fat (of which 5g saturates), 21g carbohydrate

2 tbsp olive oil

500g (1lb 2oz) pork fillet, cubed

1 medium onion, finely chopped

2 garlic cloves, finely chopped

1 tsp ground cinnamon

1 tbsp ground coriander

1 tsp ground cumin

2.5cm (1 in) piece fresh root ginger, peeled and grated

400g (14oz) canned mixed beans or chickpeas, drained

1 red pepper, deseeded and sliced

50g (2oz) ready-to-eat dried apricots, roughly chopped

300ml (½ pint) chicken stock

25g (1oz) flaked almonds, toasted

Chopped flat-leaved parsley to garnish

1 Heat 1 tbsp oil in a flameproof casserole, add the pork and fry, in batches, until brown all over. Remove and set aside. Add the remaining oil, then add the onion and cook for 10 minutes until softened. Return the pork to the casserole, add the garlic, spices and ginger and cook for 2 minutes.

2 Add the mixed beans, red pepper, apricots and stock. Season well with salt and pepper, then stir and bring to the boil. Reduce the heat to the lowest setting and simmer, covered, for 40 minutes, adding a little extra stock if it begins to looks dry. Check the seasoning and serve.

3 Sprinkle with the almonds and parsley and serve with brown basmati rice.

Venison sausages with red onion marmalade

Serves 6

Hands-on time: 15 minutes

Cooking time: 35 minutes

320 cals, 22g fat (of which 9g saturates) 20g carbohydrate per serving

12 gluten-free (100% meat) venison sausages

6 tsp redcurrant jelly

400g (14oz) red onions, peeled and chopped

2 tbsp olive oil

4 tbsp red wine vinegar

2 level tbsp demerara sugar

1 level tsp juniper berries, crushed

1 Preheat the oven to 210°C (190°C fan oven) mark 7. Put the sausages into a small roasting tin. Roast for 35 minutes, turning once.

2 After 25 minutes, spoon over the redcurrant jelly and continue to cook.

3 Meanwhile, make the red onion marmalade. Gently fry the red onions in olive oil for 15–20 minutes. Add the red wine vinegar, sugar and juniper berries, and cook for a further 5 minutes until the onions are very tender. Serve with the sausages.

▼ **COOK'S TIP**

Put some roughly cut root vegetables or parboiled potatoes, tossed in a little olive oil, in a separate roasting dish in the oven at the same time, and you have a complete meal.

Pot-roasted pheasant with red cabbage

Serves 4

Hands-on time: 20 minutes

Cooking time: 40 minutes

570 cals, 31g fat (of which 12g saturates), 15g carbohydrate per serving

25g (1oz) butter

1 tbsp oil

2 oven-ready young pheasants, halved

2 onions, peeled and sliced

450g (1lb) red cabbage, cored and finely shredded

1 tsp cornflour

250ml (8fl oz) red wine

2 tbsp redcurrant jelly

1 tbsp balsamic vinegar

4 rindless smoked streaky bacon rashers, halved

1 Preheat the oven to 200°C (180°C fan oven) mark 6. Melt the butter with the oil in a large flameproof casserole dish. Add the pheasant halves and brown on all sides, then remove and set aside. Add the onions and cabbage to the casserole dish, and fry for 5 minutes, stirring frequently, until softened.

2 Blend the cornflour with a little water, and add to the casserole with the wine, redcurrant jelly, vinegar and seasoning. Bring to the boil, stirring.

3 Arrange the pheasant halves, skin-side up, on the cabbage. Lay the halved bacon rashers on top. Cover the casserole and cook for 30 minutes or until tender (older pheasants would take an extra 10–20 minutes).

4 Serve the pot-roasted pheasant and red cabbage with the cooking juices spooned over it.

Lean lamb and tomato gratin

Serves 4

Hands-on time: 20 minutes

Cooking time: 1 hour 40 minutes

490 cals, 24g fat (of which 10g saturates), 23g carbohydrate per serving

450g (1lb) ripe tomatoes, chopped

900g (2lb) lean casserole lamb

1 tbsp olive oil

1 large onion, finely chopped

2 garlic cloves, crushed

4 level tbsp chopped parsley

2 bay leaves

125g (4oz) fresh white gluten-free breadcrumbs

1 Preheat the oven to 180°C (160°C fan oven) mark 4.

2 Trim any fat off the lamb and season. Heat the oil in a large casserole dish and brown the lamb in batches, then transfer to a plate.

3 Add the onion and garlic to the casserole dish and cook for 5 minutes, stirring occasionally, until softened. Return the lamb to the casserole, scatter with half the parsley and stir well. Spoon the tomatoes evenly over the top and season. Push in the bay leaves. Cover and bake for 1¹/₂ hours or until the lamb is tender. Preheat the grill to high.

4 Remove the bay leaves. Mix the breadcrumbs with the remaining parsley and season. Sprinkle over the lamb and grill, uncovered, for 3–5 minutes or until golden.

One-pot chicken

Serves 6

Hands-on time: 20 minutes

Cooking time: about 1 hour 40 minutes

410 cals, 29g fat (of which 9g saturates), 11g carbohydrate per serving

2 tbsp olive oil

1 large onion, cut into wedges

2 rindless streaky bacon rashers, chopped

1.6kg (3½lb) organic or free-range chicken

6 medium carrots

2 small turnips, cut into wedges

1 garlic clove, crushed

Bouquet garni (1 bay leaf, few parsley and thyme sprigs)

600ml (1 pint) hot chicken stock

100ml (3½fl oz) dry white wine

12 button mushrooms

3 tbsp chopped flat-leafed parsley

1 Heat the oil in a non-stick flameproof casserole dish, then add the onion and bacon and fry for 5 minutes until golden. Remove and set aside.

2 Add the whole chicken to the casserole and fry for 10 minutes, turning carefully to brown all over. Remove and set aside.

3 Add the carrots, turnips and garlic to the casserole and fry for 5 minutes

4 Return the bacon and onion, then put the chicken back in. Add the bouquet garni, stock and wine. Season with salt and pepper. Bring to a simmer, then cover and cook in the oven at 200°C (180°C fan oven) mark 6 for 30 minutes.

5 Remove the casserole from the oven and add the mushrooms. Baste the chicken, then re-cover and cook for a futher 50 minutes.

6 Stir in the chopped parsley. Lift out the chicken, carve and serve with the vegetables, cooking liquid and mashed potatoes.

Beef with beer and mushrooms

Serves 4

Hands-on time: 15 minutes

Cooking time: 2 hours 45 minutes – 3 hours

420 cals, 20g fat (of which 8g saturates), 19g carbohydrate per serving

700g (1¹/₂lb) braising steak, cut into large chunks

about 5cm (2in) across

2 tsp plain gluten-free flour

2 tbsp oil

25g (1oz) butter

2 large onions, peeled and finely sliced

225g (8oz) carrots, peeled and cut into large sticks

200ml (7fl oz) Guinness

300ml (¹/₂ pint) vegetable stock

2 tsp tomato purée

2 tsp English mustard

2 tsp light muscovado sugar

225g (8oz) large field mushrooms

1 Preheat the oven to 150°C (130°C fan oven) mark 2. Toss the meat in the flour. Heat the oil and butter in a large casserole dish over a medium heat and brown the meat, a few pieces at a time, removing it with a slotted spoon. The flavour and colour of the finished casserole depend on the meat taking on a good deep colour now. Stir the onion into the casserole and cook for about 10 minutes.

2 Return all the meat to the casserole, add the carrots, then stir in the Guinness, stock, tomato purée, mustard, sugar and plenty of seasoning. Bring to the boil, stir well, then cover tightly with foil or a lid and simmer gently in the oven for 1¹/₂ hours.

3 Stir the whole mushrooms into the casserole and return to the oven for a further 45 minutes – 1 hour until the meat is meltingly tender. Serve with mashed potatoes.

Curried lamb with lentils

Serves 4

Hands-on time: 15 minutes, plus marinating time

Cooking time: 1 hour 50 minutes

340 cals, 16g fat (of which 5g saturates), 14g carbohydrate per serving

500g (1lb 2oz) Welsh or British lean stewing lamb on
   the bone, cut into 8 pieces (ask your butcher to do
   this), trimmed of fat

1 level tsp ground cumin

1 level tsp ground turmeric

2 garlic cloves, peeled and crushed

1 medium red chilli (see page 74), deseeded
   and chopped

2.5cm (1in) piece fresh root ginger, grated

2 tbsp rapeseed oil

1 onion, peeled and chopped

400g (14oz) canned chopped tomatoes

2 tbsp vinegar

175g (6oz) red lentils, rinsed

Chopped coriander leaves, to serve

1 Put the lamb into a shallow sealable container, add the spices, garlic, chilli, ginger and seasoning. Stir well to mix, then cover and chill for at least 30 minutes.

2 Heat the oil in a large, flameproof casserole dish, add the onion and cook over a low heat for 5 minutes. Add the lamb and cook for 10 minutes, turning regularly, until the meat is evenly browned.

3 Add the chopped tomatoes, vinegar, 450ml (³/₄ pint) boiling water, and lentils, and bring to the boil. Reduce the heat, cover and simmer for 1 hour. Remove the lid and cook for 30 minutes, stirring occasionally, until the sauce is thick and the lamb is tender. Serve.

Braised lamb shanks with cannellini beans

Serves 6

Hands-on time: 15 minutes

Cooking time: about 3 hours

590 cals, 29g fat (of which 12g saturates), 20g carbohydrate per serving

3 tbsp olive oil

6 lamb shanks

1 large onion, chopped

3 carrots, sliced

3 celery sticks, sliced

2 garlic cloves, rushed

2 × 400g (14oz) cans chopped tomatoes

125ml (4fl oz) balsamic vinegar

2 bay leaves

2 × 410g (14$\frac{1}{4}$oz) cans cannellini beans,
   drained and rinsed

1 Preheat the oven to 170°C (150°C fan oven) mark 3. Heat the olive oil in a large, flameproof casserole dish and brown the lamb shanks, in two batches, all over. Remove and set aside.

2 Add the onion, carrots, celery and garlic to the casserole dish and cook gently until softened and just beginning to colour.

3 Return the lamb to the casserole and add the chopped tomatoes and balsamic vinegar, giving the mixture a good stir. Season with salt and pepper and add the bay leaves. Bring to a simmer, cover and cook on the hob for 5 minutes.

4 Transfer to the oven and cook for 1$\frac{1}{2}$– 2 hours or until the lamb shanks are nearly tender.

5 Remove the casserole from the oven and add the cannellini beans. Cover and return to the oven for a further 30 minutes. Serve with cooked spinach.

Treats

We all need treats. We have made sure, however, that ours are delicious and have a low to medium calorie count. Look no further for simple, mouthwatering ideas using fruit. You will be surprised at just how good wheat-free cakes and biscuits can be, too.

Ginger-glazed pineapple

Rhubarb fool

Griddled peaches

Apple and raspberry mousse

Nutmeg custards

Mango, blueberry and lime fruit salad

Strawberries with chocolate meringue

Dark chocolate soufflés

Chocolate cherry roll

Orange and almond cake

Fruity tea cake

Sticky lemon polenta cake

Carrot cake

Luxury chocolate orange torte

Forest fruits granita

Spiced star biscuits

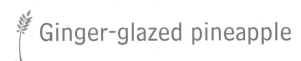

Ginger-glazed pineapple

Serves 6

Hands-on time: 10 minutes

Cooking time: 10 minutes

60 cals, 0g fat, 15g carbohydrate per serving

2 pineapples

2 tbsp light muscovado sugar

2 tsp ground ginger

1 Cut the pineapples into quarters lengthways, leaving the stalk intact. Remove the core, extract the flesh, and reserve the skin. Cut the flesh into pieces and return to the pineapple shell. Wrap the green leaves of the stalk in foil.

2 Preheat the grill. Mix together the sugar and ginger. Sprinkle each pineapple quarter with the sugar mixture. Put on foil-lined baking sheets and grill for 10 minutes until golden and caramelized. Serve with natural yogurt and a drizzle of runny honey.

▼ **COOK'S TIP**

This is the perfect dessert after a heavy or rich meal. Fresh pineapple contains an enzyme, bromelin, which digests protein very effectively and helps balance any excess acidity or alkalinity. Ginger is a well-known digestive and has many therapeutic properties.

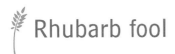

Rhubarb fool

Serves 6

Hands-on time: 5 minutes, plus chilling time

Cooking time: 10 minutes

60 cals, 0g fat, 14g carbohydrate per serving

450g (1lb) rhubarb, thickly chopped

50ml (2fl oz) orange juice

1 cinnamon stick

25g (1oz) golden caster sugar

1 tbsp redcurrant jelly

150ml ($^1/_4$ pint) fat-free Greek-style yogurt

2 tbsp soft brown sugar

1 Put the rhubarb, orange juice, cinnamon stick and caster sugar into a pan. Cover and cook gently for 10 minutes or until tender.

2 Remove the lid and cook for 5 minutes until the liquid has evaporated. Discard the cinnamon stick. Stir in the redcurrant jelly then leave to cool.

3 Roughly fold in the yogurt, then spoon the mixture into six glasses and sprinkle with the soft brown sugar. Chill for 2 hours.

 Griddled peaches

Serves 4

Hands-on time: 15 minutes

Cooking time: 6–8 minutes

100 cals, 5g fat (of which 1g saturates), 12g carbohydrate per serving

4 ripe but firm peaches

1 tbsp maple syrup

1 tsp light olive oil

25g (1oz) pecan nuts, toasted

1 Halve the peaches and carefully remove the stones. Cut the flesh into thick slices, then put into a bowl with the maple syrup and toss to coat.

2 Heat the oil in a griddle or large frying pan, add the peaches and cook for 3–4 minutes on each side until starting to char and caramelize. Sprinkle with the toasted pecan nuts and serve at once.

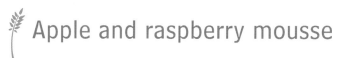

Apple and raspberry mousse

Serves 6

Hands-on time: 10 minutes, plus chilling

Cooking time: about 15 minutes

120 cals, 0g fat, 31g carbohydrate per serving

900g (2lb) cooking apples, peeled, cored and sliced

4 tbsp orange juice

Grated zest of 1 organic lemon

225g (8oz) raspberries

6 tbsp golden caster sugar

1 large egg white

Mint sprigs, to decorate

1 Put the apples and orange juice into a pan and cook over a low heat, uncovered, for 10 minutes until soft. Add the lemon zest, then use a fork to mash to a purée. Cover and chill for at least 1 hour.

2 Gently heat the raspberries and 2 tbsp sugar in a pan until the juices start to run.

3 Whisk the egg white in a clean, grease-free bowl until stiff, adding the remaining sugar gradually until the mixture forms stiff peaks. Fold into the apple purée.

4 Divide the raspberries and any juice among six serving glasses, spoon the apple mixture on top and decorate with mint sprigs.

Nutmeg custards

Serves 6

Hands-on time: 10 minutes

Cooking time: 50 minutes, plus cooling time

120 cals, 5g fat (of which 1g saturates), 12g carbohydrate per serving

450ml (¾ pint) skimmed milk

3 tbsp golden caster sugar

4 eggs

¼ tsp ground nutmeg

5 tbsp low-fat fromage frais

Freshly grated nutmeg, to decorate

1 Preheat the oven to 170°C (150°C fan oven) mark 3. Heat the milk with the caster sugar in a pan until dissolved. Leave to cool.

2 Put the eggs, ground nutmeg and fromage frais into a bowl and whisk in the cooled milk. Strain the mixture into six individual ramekins, then carefully put them into a roasting tin. Add enough hot water to come halfway up the sides of the ramekins, then cover the tin with foil and bake for 45 minutes.

3 Leave the custards to cool, then decorate with freshly grated nutmeg. Serve.

Mango, blueberry and lime fruit salad

Serves 4

Hands-on time: 10 minutes

Cooking time: none

per serving: 130 cals, 0g fat, 32g carbohydrate

2 organic oranges

1 mango

450g (1lb) peeled and diced fresh pineapple

200g (7oz) blueberries

1/2 Charentais melon, cubed

Zest and juice of 1 organic lime

1 Using a sharp knife, peel the oranges, remove the pith and cut into segments. Put into a bowl.

2 Cut down the length of the mango and cut around the stone to remove as much flesh as possible. Scoop out the flesh from the two halves and chop. Add to the bowl with the pineapple chunks and blueberries.

3 Add the melon cubes, lime zest and juice, and mix together. Serve immediately.

Strawberries with chocolate meringue

Serves 6

Hands-on time: 15 minutes

Cooking time: 20–25 minutes

120 cals, 1g fat (of which trace saturates), 27g carbohydrate per serving

225g (8oz) strawberries, chopped

Finely grated zest of $\frac{1}{2}$ organic orange

125g (4oz) caster sugar, plus 1 tbsp extra

3 large egg white

1 tbsp cocoa powder

15g ($\frac{1}{2}$oz) hazelnuts, toasted and chopped

1 Preheat the oven to 150°C (130°C fan oven) mark 2. Mix together the strawberries, orange zest and 1 tbsp caster sugar. Divide among six ramekins.

2 Put the egg whites into a clean, grease-free bowl and whisk until soft peaks form. Add the remaining sugar and whisk until the whites are stiff and shiny. Fold in the cocoa.

3 Spoon the chocolate meringue over the fruit and sprinkle the hazelnuts on top.

4 Bake in the oven for 20–25 minutes or until the meringue is crisp on the outside and soft in the middle. Serve immediately.

Dark chocolate soufflés

Serves 6
Hands-on time: 20 minutes
Cooking time: about 20 minutes
150 cals, 5g fat (of which 3g saturates), 21g carbohydrate per serving

50g (2oz) dark plain chocolate
   (70% cocoa solids), chopped

2 tbsp cornflour

1 tbsp cocoa powder

1 tsp instant coffee granules

4 tbsp golden caster sugar

150ml ($^{1}/_{4}$ pint) skimmed milk

2 eggs, separated, plus 1 egg white

Golden icing sugar, to dust

1 Preheat the oven to 190°C (170°C fan oven) mark 5 and heat a baking sheet. Put the chocolate into a pan with the cornflour, cocoa, coffee, 1 tbsp caster sugar and the milk, and warm gently to melt the chocolate. Increase the heat and stir until the mixture thickens. Leave to cool a little, then stir in the egg yolks. Cover with damp greaseproof paper.

2 Whisk the egg whites in a clean, grease-free bowl until soft peaks form. Gradually whisk in the remaining sugar until the mixture is stiff.

3 Stir one-third of the egg whites into the chocolate mixture, then fold in the remaining whites and divide among six ramekins.

4 Bake in oven for 12 minutes. Dust with icing sugar and serve immediately.

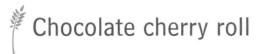

Chocolate cherry roll

Serves 6–8

Hands-on time: 30 minutes

Cooking time: 30 minutes, plus cooling time

190 cals, 6g fat (of which 2g saturates), 27g carbohydrate per serving

4 tbsp cocoa powder, plus extra to dust

100ml (3½fl oz) milk, plus 3 tbsp extra

5 eggs, separated

125g (4oz) golden caster sugar

400g (14oz) canned cherries without stones

1–2 tbsp cherry jam

Icing sugar, to dust

1 Preheat the oven to 180°C (160°C fan oven) mark 4. Line a 30 × 20cm (12 × 8in) Swiss roll tin with baking parchment. In a bowl, mix together the cocoa and 3 tbsp milk. Heat 100ml (3½fl oz) milk in a pan until almost boiling, then add to the bowl, stirring. Leave to cool for 10 minutes.

2 Whisk the egg whites in a clean, grease-free bowl until soft peaks form. In a separate bowl, whisk together the egg yolks and caster sugar until pale and thick. Gradually whisk in the cooled milk, then fold in the egg whites. Spoon the mixture into the prepared tin and smooth the surface.

3 Bake in the oven for 25 minutes or until just firm. Turn out on to a board lined with baking parchment and peel off the lining parchment. Cover with a damp tea towel.

4 Drain the cherries and chop the fruit. Spread the jam over the sponge and top with the cherries. Roll up from the shortest end, dust with cocoa and icing sugar, then cut into slices and serve.

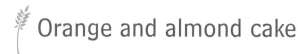

Orange and almond cake

Serves 10

Hands-on time: 20 minutes

Cooking time: 40 minutes

180 cals, 9g fat (of which 1g saturates), 20g carbohydrate per serving

Butter, to grease

50g (2oz) rice flour

Juice of 3 organic oranges (200ml/7fl oz)

Grated rind of 1 organic orange

125g (4oz) ground almonds

1 tbsp orange-flower water (if available)

4 medium eggs, separated

$1/4$ tsp salt

125g (4oz) caster sugar

1 Preheat the oven to 180°C (160°C fan oven) mark 4. Grease and line a 23cm (9in) square cake tin. Mix together the rice flour, orange juice and orange rind, then add the ground almonds and orange-flower water.

2 Beat the egg yolks with the sugar and $1/4$ tsp salt in a bowl until almost white. Add to the first mixture. Beat the egg whites until stiff, then fold into the cake mixture. Spoon into the prepared cake tin and bake in the oven for about 40 minutes. Leave to cool in the tin.

3 When cold, turn the cake out.

▼ **COOK'S TIP**

For a festive occasion top with whipped cream and sprinkle with silver balls.

Fruity tea cake

Serves 12

Hands-on time: 20 minutes, plus soaking time

Cooking time: 1 hour

190 cals, 1g fat (of which trace saturates), 44g carbohydrate per serving

150ml (¹/₄ pint) hot tea, made with

  2 Earl Grey teabags

200g (7oz) sultanas

75g (3oz) ready-to-eat dried figs, roughly chopped

75g (3oz) ready-to-eat prunes, roughly chopped

A little vegetable oil, to oil

125g (4oz) dark muscovado sugar

2 medium eggs, beaten

225g (8oz) gluten-free flour

2 tsp wheat-free baking powder

2 level tsp ground mixed spice

1 Pour the tea into a bowl and add the dried fruit. Leave to soak for 30 minutes.

2 Preheat the oven to 190°C (170°C fan oven) mark 5. Oil a 900g (2lb) loaf tin and line the base with greaseproof paper.

3 In a large bowl, beat together the muscovado sugar and eggs until pale and slightly thickened. Add the flour, baking powder, ground mixed spice and soaked dried fruit and tea, then mix together well.

4 Spoon the mixture into the prepared loaf tin and bake in the centre of the oven for 45 minutes – 1 hour. Leave to cool.

5 Serve sliced, with a little butter if you want to. Wrap in clingfilm and store in an airtight container. It will keep for up to five days.

Sticky lemon polenta cake

Serves 12

Hands-on time: 10 minutes

Cooking time: 1 hour, plus cooling time

190 cals, 6g fat (of which 3g saturates), 36g carbohydrate per serving

50g (2oz) softened butter, plus extra for greasing

3 organic lemons

250g (9oz) golden caster sugar

250g (9oz) instant polenta

1 tsp baking powder

2 large eggs

50ml (2fl oz) semi-skimmed milk

2 tbsp natural yogurt

2 tbsp poppy seeds

1 Preheat the oven to 180°C (160°C fan oven) mark 4. Lightly grease and line the base of a 900g (2lb) loaf tin.

2 Zest 1 lemon and put into a food processor with the butter, 200g (7oz) sugar, the polenta, baking powder, eggs, milk, yogurt and poppy seeds and whiz until smooth.

3 Spoon the mixture into the prepared tin and smooth the top. Bake in the oven for 55 minutes – 1 hour or until a skewer inserted into the centre comes out clean. Leave to cool in the tin for 10 minutes.

4 Next, make a syrup. Squeeze the juice from the zested lemon plus 1 more lemon. Thinly slice the third lemon. Put into a pan with the remaining sugar and 150ml (1/4 pint) water. Bring to the boil and bubble for about 10 minutes until syrupy, then remove from the heat.

5 Slide a knife around the edge of the cake and turn out on to a serving plate. Pierce the cake in several places with a skewer, spoon the syrup over it and decorate with lemon slices. Wrap in clingfilm and store in an airtight container for up to 3 days.

Carrot cake

Serves 12

Hands-on time: 20 minutes

Cooking time: 1 hour, plus cooling time

190 cals, 6g fat (of which 1g saturates), 30g carbohydrate per serving

1 tsp oil, to oil

150ml (5fl oz) prune juice

175g (6oz) light muscovado sugar

4 eggs, separated

Finely grated rind of $1/2$ organic orange

2 tsp lemon juice

175g (6oz) gluten-free flour, sifted

$1^1/_2$ level tsp baking powder

75g (3oz) ground almonds

350g (12oz) carrots, peeled and coarsely grated

1 Preheat the oven to 180°C (160°C fan oven) mark 4. Grease and line the base of a deep 20cm (8in) round cake tin.

2 In a large bowl, mix together the prune juice and sugar. Beat in the egg yolks, orange rind and lemon juice.

3 Sift the flour and baking powder into the mixture, then fold in the almonds and grated carrots.

4 Whisk the egg whites in a clean bowl until stiff, then fold into the cake mixture. Pour into the prepared cake tin.

5 Bake the cake in the oven for about 1 hour or until risen and firm. Leave in the tin for 10 minutes, then turn out on to a wire rack to cool completely.

Luxury chocolate orange torte

Serves 12

Hands-on time: 30 minutes

Cooking time: 55 minutes – 1 hour 5 minutes

280 cals, 18g fat (of which 7g saturates), 23g carbohydrate per serving

75g (3oz) butter, diced, plus extra to grease

100g (3½oz) plain chocolate (at least 70% cocoa
  solids), broken into pieces

6 medium eggs

225g (8oz) golden caster sugar

150g (5oz) ground almonds, sifted

Zest and juice of 1 organic orange

1 Preheat the oven to 190°C (170°C fan oven) mark 5. Grease a 20cm (8in) springform cake tin and line with greaseproof paper.

2 Melt the chocolate and butter in a bowl set over a pan of gently simmering water. Remove the bowl from the pan and set aside to cool a little.

3 Put the eggs and sugar into a large bowl and mix with an electric hand whisk until the volume has tripled and the mixture is thick and foamy – it will take about 5–10 minutes.

4 Add the ground almonds, orange zest and juice to the egg mixture, then gently fold together with a metal spoon.

5 Pour about two-thirds of the mixture into the prepared cake tin. Add the melted chocolate and butter to the remaining mixture and fold together. Add to the tin and swirl around just once or twice to create a marbled effect. Bake in the oven for 50 minutes – 1 hour. Leave to cool in the tin, then carefully remove the torte and slice it.

Forest fruits granita

Serves 6

Hands-on time: 15 minutes, plus freezing time

Cooking time: 2 minutes

100 cals, 0g fat, 22g carbohydrate per serving

350g (12oz) frozen forest fruits or a mix of fresh blackberries, strawberries, redcurrants and blackcurrants

75g (3oz) golden caster sugar

150ml ($^1/_4$ pint) red wine

50ml (2fl oz) crème de cassis

Extra berries, to serve

1 Put the frozen fruit, sugar, wine, cassis and 150ml ($^1/_4$ pint) water into a pan. Bring to the boil and bubble for 3–4 minutes until softened. Fresh fruit does not need to be cooked.

2 Leave to cool, then drain, reserving the juice. Put the fruit into a blender and whiz until well broken down. Sieve to a purée and mix with the reserved juice. Pour into a shallow, freezer-proof metal container and freeze, uncovered, for 2 hours, then stir to break up the ice crystals. Cover and freeze until the mixture is just firm (about 1 hour).

3 To serve, put into the fridge for 15 minutes. Use a spoon to break down the mixture. Serve in chilled glasses with extra berries.

Spiced star biscuits

Makes about 35
Hands-on time: 15 minutes, plus chilling time
Cooking time: 15–20 minutes, plus cooling time
50 cals, 2g fat (of which trace saturates), 7g carbohydrate per biscuit

2 tbsp runny honey

25g (1oz) unsalted butter

50g (2oz) light muscovado sugar

Finely grated zest of 1/2 organic lemon

Finely grated zest of 1/2 organic orange

225g (8oz) gluten-free flour,
plus extra for dusting

1 tsp wheat-free baking powder

1 tsp ground cinnamon

1 tsp ground ginger

1/2 tsp freshly grated nutmeg

Pinch of ground cloves

Pinch of salt

1 tbsp finely chopped
candied peel

50g (2oz) ground almonds

1 large egg, beaten

2–3 tbsp milk

1 Put the honey, butter, sugar and citrus zests into a small pan and stir over a low heat until the butter has melted and the ingredients are well combined.

2 Sift the flour, baking powder, spices and salt together in a bowl, then add the chopped candied peel and ground almonds. Add the melted mixture, beaten egg and milk, and mix until the dough comes together, adding a little extra milk if the dough feels crumbly. Knead the dough briefly until smooth, then wrap in clingfilm and chill for at least 4 hours or overnight.

3 Preheat the oven to 180°C (160°C fan oven) mark 4. Roll out the dough on a lightly floured surface to a thickness of 5mm (1/4in). Stamp out stars, using a 5cm (2in) cutter, and put on several baking sheets.

4 Bake in the oven for 15–20 minutes or until just beginning to brown at the edges. Transfer the biscuits to a wire rack to cool. Store in an airtight tin for up to a week.

▼ COOK'S TIP

To decorate, coat some of the bisuits with icing and silver balls.

Contents

Useful contacts

The Coeliac Society UK
www.coeliac.co.uk
Tel: 0870 4448804
Leading charity offering advice and support to sufferers and their families. Excellent website; links include international societies, research and recipe sites, gluten free manufacturers etc.

Gluten-Free Foods Direct
www.glutenfreefoodsdirect.co.uk
Tel: 01757 700636
Online gluten and wheat free shopping.

Bread Matters Ltd
www.breadmatters.com
Tel: 01768 881899
Specialist gluten free bread and baking courses. Highly recommended.

www.inside-story.com
Website for Foods Matter, food sensitivity magazine. Excellent links section, including allergy sites.

British Allergy Foundation (Allergy UK)
www.allergyuk.org
Helpline: 01322 619898
Leading medical charity for people with allergies, intolerances and chemical sensitivities. Help, advice, contacts and an excellent website.

Author acknowledgements

First and foremost, for her guidance throughout, I should like to express my gratitude and profound thanks to my editor, Nicola Hodgson. No one could have been gentler, more patient or more co-operative. For their invaluable professional advice and help I should also like to offer my very sincere thanks to Andrew Whitley, Michelle Berriedale - Johnson, Julia Charles and the Coeliac Society. On a personal level, for Joanna and Catey, for their unstinting support and affection, and for Stephanie, for her constant encouragement and good humour, my heartfelt thanks and love.

Photographer credits

Will Heap: 45, 54, 65, 79, 89, 93, 97, 105, 115, 123, 139, 141, 149

David Munns: 153

Clive Streeter: 131

Roger Stowell: 127

Lucinda Symons: (Food Stylist: Sarah Tildesley) jacket image, 2, 4, 6, 9, 20, 22, 28, 32, 40, 50, 59, 60, 69, 73, 83, 84, 101, 109, 110, 119, 125, 135, 136.